K9 LINE-UP TRAINING

K9 Professional Training Series

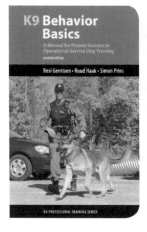

K9 Behavior Basics
A Manual for Proven Success in Operational Service Dog Training
second edition
Resi Gerritsen · Ruud Haak · Simon Prins
K9 PROFESSIONAL TRAINING SERIES

K9 Drug Detection
A Manual for Training and Operations
Resi Gerritsen · Ruud Haak
K9 PROFESSIONAL TRAINING SERIES

K9 Scent Training
A Manual for Training Your Identification, Tracking and Detection Dog
Resi Gerritsen · Ruud Haak
K9 PROFESSIONAL TRAINING SERIES

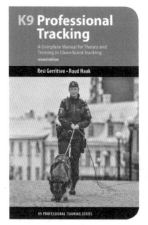

K9 Professional Tracking
A Complete Manual for Theory and Training in Clean-Scent Tracking
second edition
Resi Gerritsen · Ruud Haak
K9 PROFESSIONAL TRAINING SERIES

K9 Explosive and Mine Detection
A Manual for Training and Operations
Resi Gerritsen · Ruud Haak
K9 PROFESSIONAL TRAINING SERIES

K9 Schutzhund Training
A Manual for IGP Training through Positive Reinforcement
Updated second edition
Resi Gerritsen · Ruud Haak
K9 PROFESSIONAL TRAINING SERIES

See the complete list at
dogtrainingpress.com

K9 LINE-UP TRAINING

A Manual for Suspect Identification and Detection Work

Dr. Resi Gerritsen, Ruud Haak,
and Simon Prins

An imprint of
Brush Education Inc.

Brush Education is located on Treaty 6 territory and is a beneficiary of this treaty. We gratefully acknowledge this land and the many peoples—including the Nêhiyawak, Anishninaabe, Niitsitapi, Saulteaux, Métis, Dene, Nakota Isga, Nakota Sioux, and Inuit—for whom this land continues to be a traditional home, meeting ground, gathering place, and travelling route.

Brush Education Inc.

www.brusheducation.ca

contact@brusheducation.ca

This book is available in print, PDF, and Global Certified Acessible™ EPUB formats.

Parts of this book are drawn from Ruud Haak's contributions to *K9 Suspect Discrimination: Training and Practicing Scent Identification Line-Ups*, by Adee Schoon and Ruud Haak (Detselig Enterprises, 2002).

Cover design: John Luckhurst; Cover image: Dog Training Center Oosterhout
Interior design: Carol Dragich, Dragich Design

Library and Archives Canada Cataloguing in Publication

Title: K9 line-up training : a manual for suspect identification and detection work / Dr. Resi Gerritsen, Ruud Haak, and Simon Prins.

Names: Gerritsen, Resi, author. | Haak, Ruud, 1947- author. | Prins, Simon, 1967- author.

Description: Series statement: K9 professional training series | Includes bibliographical references.

Identifiers: Canadiana (print) 20220468486 | Canadiana (ebook) 20220468516 | ISBN 9781550599275 (softcover) | ISBN 9781550599299 (EPUB) | ISBN 9781550599282 (PDF)

Subjects: LCSH: Detector dogs—Training. | LCSH: Detector dogs—Sense organs. | LCSH: Olfactory sensors.

Classification: LCC SF428.73 .G46 2023 | DDC 636.73–dc23

Contents

Preface

K9 nose work for suspect discrimination or substance detection has long been a tool in the forensic investigator's tool kit. In recent decades, detection work in particular has expanded worldwide, and dogs have increasingly been used to detect everything from drugs to explosives, missing people to electronic storage devices, money to biohazards. The hobbyist has also discovered the fun of training dogs in detection of household smells and the discrimination and identification of particular people's scents.

In every context, a well-trained and reliable K9 nose is a most important asset. A dog's nose is an incredible thing—you can learn more about that in Resi and Ruud's book *K9 Professional Tracking*, now in its second edition. But even for this incredible nose, scent and odor work can be incredibly challenging, especially without the right training. Yet there is little knowledge out there about the different methods of training dogs in scent identification and detection, and even less about the ways that that training can go wrong. That's why we've written this book: so this knowledge is accessible to all dog handlers who want to know more about it.

This book introduces both professional and amateur dog handlers to the basics of scent and odor line-up training and their applications, current and historical, in K9 scent identification and detection work. From training schedules to the fascinating history of nose work in Dutch policing, we've designed this book to be a practical, accessible, informative, and at times entertaining resource for K9 officers, professional or volunteer search-and-rescue workers, competitive dog trainers, and enthusiastic hobbyists alike.

All three of us are from the Netherlands, and have spent our K9 careers here. Our perspectives on dog training and detection line-up work are thus steeped in the Dutch context, with its long

and interesting history of K9 detection work. We believe that this
context and history, which we go into especially in the chapters on
scent identification, will not only be interesting to the K9 detection enthusiast, but will contribute important insights into the
possibilities and pitfalls of this work. We hope that this English-
language book on the topic will help bring all detection dog handlers, together with their dogs, to a higher level of training and
expertise.

DR. RESI GERRITSEN, RUUD HAAK, AND SIMON PRINS

DISCLAIMER

While the contents of this book are based on substantial experience and expertise,
working with dogs involves inherent risks, especially in dangerous settings and situations.
Anyone using approaches described in this book does so entirely at their own risk and
both the author and publisher disclaim any liability for any injuries or other damage that
may be sustained.

Introduction

This is a book about K9 line-up training—but what is a line-up? For our purposes in this book, when we use the term *line-up*, we are referring to a series of scents or odors presented to a dog in one or more rows, a pattern, or a circle, with the goal of gaining information about these scents and odors from the dog's behavior, in particular the presence or absence of a response or alert behavior. We don't use *scent* and *odor* here as synonyms, but rather give them precise meanings. A scent is the smell of a live human being, while an odor is the smell of a nonhuman being or substance.[1] We use the word *smell* when no special distinction is necessary.

Depending on the context of the line-up, the scents and odors present may be of different strengths or purities, and may be familiar or unfamiliar to the dog. Line-ups are used to train and test dogs in both suspect identification and scent and odor detection. In the context of detection, line-ups are invaluable to the challenging process of imprinting specific odors onto the dog in a way that will be useful and reliable in working environments. They are also used in sport detection contexts and for some certification processes. When it comes to suspect identification, standardized scent line-ups are used not only in training, but also at work. The point of these line-ups is to learn something from the dog about the scents present. Specifically, does one of them match the target scent we've given the dog?

This information can be incredibly valuable. It can tell us, for example, whether the scent of a particular person matches a scent found at a crime scene, or whether an area smells of explosive material. In some cases, and depending on your jurisdiction, this information can be used as supporting evidence in courts of law. This information is only valuable, however, if we know that it's reliable—and reliable scent and odor work take careful, consistent, and rigorous training. That's what this book is all about.

What Can Dogs Smell—and What Can't They?

A dog's nose is many times more sensitive than that of a human being. They are capable of detecting scents and odors at much lower concentrations than we can, and of distinguishing individual smells from within complex mixtures. With practice, dogs can hone their natural ability and learn to communicate to us what they perceive.[2]

When trained correctly, a dog can give us information about a situation—a crime scene or piece of evidence, for example—that we would otherwise have no access to. It can give us information about the scents or odors that it can smell, but we cannot. However, a dog cannot tell us definitively whether someone whose scent they smell has actually committed a crime. Nor can a dog tell us if explosives are actually present at a scene, or if the odor of explosives is simply lingering there. When working in scent identification or scent and odor detection, it is absolutely crucial that you always remember what a dog can smell, and what it cannot. It can smell scents and odors—the volatile chemicals emitted by humans, objects, and substances—whether they are coming directly from their source or deposited somewhere else. They cannot tell you what the presence of those scents or odors means.

Think of it like a fingerprint analysis. If a person's fingerprint is found on a glass at a crime scene, this proves that the person held the glass, not that the person is responsible for the murder that took place in the room where the glass was found. If the fingerprint is found on the murder weapon, it proves that the person held this weapon and that any subsequent handling has not erased his traces. This second situation is obviously more relevant than the first, but is still not conclusive evidence that this person committed the crime. More evidence is needed.

The same is true in scent and odor work, especially in working contexts. It is essential to remember this fact: Dogs can support an investigation, but they cannot *solve* it.

Avoiding Handler Influence

It is also essential for professionals and amateurs to understand that just because a dog *can* use its nose doesn't mean it will. Dogs—especially well-trained dogs—are masters of observing and interpreting human behavior. They use human beings as a source of information that is as important as, if not more important than, all other sources of information in their environment. The handler, without realizing it, is sending information to the dog about where and how the dog can get reinforcement. Indeed, dogs are opportunistic animals. They will try to get their reinforcements quickly, and in the shortest and most accessible way. If that means scanning the body language of the handler, the instructor, or even bystanders, they will—and often, the humans are none the wiser.

This becomes a problem when you are asking a dog to use its nose to confirm something about a scent or odor that you or someone else visible to the dog already knows or believes they already know. We call this type of influence the Clever Hans effect.

THE CLEVER HANS EFFECT

Dogs are not the only animals that are capable of using humans' unconscious body language to their own benefit. Horses can too. One horse in particular famously pulled the wool over the eyes of everyone who saw him perform, including his trainer. This horse's name was *Kluger Hans*, or Clever Hans.[3]

Clever Hans lived in Germany at the turn of the twentieth century. His owner, Wilhelm von Osten, was an eccentric man with a fervent belief. He believed horse to be at least as intelligent as human beings. Indeed, he was absolutely convinced that horse could be taught to count, read, and perform simple mathematical equations, among other things—and he was determined to prove it.

Figure 0.1 Wilhelm von Osten training his stallion, Clever Hans.

His first challenge was to teach Hans how to communicate his own thoughts to humans—that is, to teach him a language of sorts. After careful consideration, von Osten chose to teach Hans how to tap his front hoof in response to questions. All letters in the alphabet and every number were translated into specific numbers of hoof taps. To train Hans in this language, von Osten would say a number or letter or ask a question, then take Hans's leg in his hands and tap out the correct response. The horse eventually learned to move his leg without help. After some time, the animal seemed to understand this language, and to use it to correctly respond to von Osten's questions.

On June 28, 1902, von Osten placed an advertisement in a newspaper that read: "I want to sell my seven-year-old, fine, docile stallion with which I do tests in order to determine the intellectual powers of a horse. The horse distinguishes ten colors, reads, knows the four main processes of calculation, and a lot more."[4] Von Osten did not really want to sell Hans. Rather, his advertisement was meant to garner interest in his marvelous horse, and to convince people of the truth of his opinion that the intelligence of animals such as horses is equal to that of human beings. At first, to the annoyance of von Osten, people dismissed the ad as a joke. Only after he placed a second ad did he begin to receive responses. Now it was time to show off Hans's amazing abilities.

Von Osten invited a select group of guests to interact with Hans and interrogate him. The horse, the audience found, knew a lot. Hans could name the date, tell what time it was, convert fractions into decimals, add, subtract, multiply, and divide. The audience was amazed. News of Clever Hans went around the country, and then around the world. Some enthusiastically welcomed the news as proof of animal intelligence, while others were more suspicious, believing Hans's performance to be somehow fraudulent. Even to the animal psychologists of the time, Clever Hans's behavior was a mystery. Indeed, some of the leading scientists in the field, after examining Hans, declined to make any solid conclusions about the horse's behavior or intelligence (though they did note that they did not detect the kinds of tricks usually used with performing circus animals). The hesitation of these top scientists shows just how real Hans's skills appeared to be.

Figure 0.2 Wilhelm von Osten performing with Clever Hans.

In the end, the miraculous abilities of Clever Hans were shown to be nothing more than an illusion—albeit an unintentional one on the part of von Osten. When Oskar Pfungst, another animal psychologist, came to examine Hans at work, he also, wisely, examined the behavior of von Osten and others who asked Hans questions. Pfungst looked at their body language and how they might be communicating with Hans, even without knowing it.

It was clear to Pfungst that this was not a case of fraud—not some magic trick surreptitiously passed off as real. After all, Pfungst himself had questioned the horse while von Osten was not visible, and Hans had correctly answered the questions with his hoof. For a person—including a trainer—without animal psychological training, there would be no doubt that the horse could indeed think and do math. But Pfungst was not convinced. He performed several new experiments, including trials in which Hans could see neither the person asking the question nor the other spectators present, and trials in which the questioner and spectators did not know the answer to the question being asked. In these experiments, the stallion would start tapping his hoof, but would not stop. As Pfungst wrote, "The animal seemed to be confused."[5] It was soon clear that the stallion was waiting for a cue from someone in the room to stop tapping, but no one could give this sign, either because the horse could not see them or because they didn't know the answer. Pfungst concluded:

> So far as I can see, the following explanation is the only one that will comport with these facts: The horse must have learned, in the course of the long period of problem-solving, to attend ever more closely, while tapping, to the slight changes in bodily posture with which the master unconsciously accompanied the steps in his own thought-processes, and to use these as closing signals. The motive for this direction and straining of attention was the regular reward, in the form of carrots and bread, which attended it. This unexpected kind of independent activity and the

certainty and precision of the perception of minimal movements thus attained are astounding in the highest degree.

The movements that call forth the horse's reaction are
so extremely slight in the case of Mr. von Osten that it is
easily comprehensible how it was possible that they should
escape the notice even of practiced observers.[6]

Note that Pfungst's conclusion is not that Hans was not
intelligent—not at all. Rather, he discovered Hans's incredible
capacity to problem-solve using his highly acute ability to observe
human behaviors of which humans themselves were unaware.
Hans's "correct answers" were in fact learned reactions to the small,
unconscious movements made by his questioners as soon as they
were satisfied with his tapped-out response. Hans used this information as a cue to stop tapping.

HUMANS ARE A SOURCE OF INFORMATION
Clever Hans is still of importance today for animal trainers, particularly dog trainers. Dogs are very opportunistic animals and they
pay a lot of attention to our body language. Often, based on our
subtle physical cues, they can predict when the reinforcement is
about to come, and use this extra information as confirmation. We
can't hide our body signals from our dogs.

As Hungarian scientist Dr. Ádám Miklósi proved in his 1998
study on this subject, dogs seem to be able to learn physical cues
even faster than Clever Hans did.[7] Miklósi confirmed that dogs
both perceive and make use of cues such as pointing, bowing, nod-
ding, head turning, and glancing. In 2002, Krisztina Soproni and
her colleagues deepened this research by testing the dog's responsiveness to human pointing gestures. The study involved several
different tests to determine if exposure to a pointing gesture made
dogs more able to find a hidden treat. The observations were carried out in each of the dogs' owners' apartments, with only Soproni,
the owner, and the dog present. Soproni et al. found that in tests
where the dogs were able to see a pointing hand, and even those

in which they were able to see the body language and position of someone pointing without being able to see the hand itself, dogs performed better than dumb luck, finding the hidden kibble more often than would otherwise be expected. Soproni's team concluded that the dogs were able to interpret and respond to relatively novel pointing gestures, and they were able to comprehend the referential nature of human pointing to some extent.[8]

In 2011, Lit, Schweitzer, and Oberbauer showed us how difficult it is for handlers to avoid influencing their dogs. They found that, even when the handlers were trying to avoid doing so, and even when they were aware of the purpose of the study, they continued to have an influence on their dog's performance.[9] In the study, explosives and narcotics dog-and-handler teams were asked to do a series of building searches. One of the odors hidden in the building was marked with a paper marker. Experimenters asked handlers to ignore this marker, but told them that the marker indicated the location of a target scent. This was, however, not the case. In every experimental condition, none of the odors used were narcotics or explosives odors. In other words, any alert that a dog made would be incorrect.

Considering there was no target odor, we would expect handlers to report no alerts, at the very least, no preference in the dog for a particular odor. Instead, handlers reported that their dogs alerted more at the marked odor than at any other odor. The result very clearly showed that handlers were influenced by "clues" like the paper marker, and that their beliefs about the odors' positions influenced their dogs' performances.

HUMAN INFLUENCE IN K9 LINE-UPS

Clearly, the influence a dog handler can have on her dog is a big issue. In the context of training nose work, this means that you cannot expect the dog to focus on its scents or odors and simply ignore you, the handler. When a handler knows or even believes she knows where a target odor is hidden or which scent will match a piece of evidence, she sets herself up for failure: her body language is telling the dog what she expects it to do. When those around the dog have too much knowledge about the contents of a line-up, the dog will stop using his nose and mind and start using you to solve the line-up.

Any kind of cue that precedes a behavior in a dog is called an *antecedent*. Some antecedents are environmental, like a cat running by and causing the dog to give chase. Others are from the handler or other people near the dog. These can be intentional, like giving the command "search," or unintentional. Imagine a dog is performing a scent identification line-up and is approaching the suspect's scent. The trainer, who knows the position of this scent, is already reaching for the reinforcement in his pocket. When the dog sees the trainer's hand moving toward the reinforcement, the dog know a reinforcement is on its way. The hand moving to the pocket, the sound of a Velcro strap, a change in the handler's voice, taking a position behind the dog—all of these often unconscious cues tell the dog that reinforcement is about to come.

The handler is not the only person who may influence a dog's performance. The person who sets up a particular training trial, and thus knows the location of decoys and target scents, can be an important source of information to a dog, as can any spectators who are in the know. When those spectators stop moving, stop talking, or lean in with bated breath, the dog will quickly understand that he is near the hidden odor or target scent.

In some cases, antecedents produce the Clever Hans effect: the dog alerts or responds because it knows that's what it needs to do to get a reinforcement, not because it has correctly identified the target scent. In other cases, antecedents interfere with basic training: a dog that is about to alert, for example, may run toward its handler for its reward instead of completing and persevering in its alert.

A LITTLE "FIE!"

A scent identification line-up played an important role in a 1968 court case concerning the murder of a pub owner in the Dutch village of Oirschot.* One man quickly became the prime suspect. As part of their investigation, officers performed a scent identification line-up using the suspect's scent and a number of decoys. The handler who conducted the line-up knew the position of the suspect's scent. When he saw his dog intended to respond to one of the decoy scents, he corrected his dog by quietly saying, "fie." The dog stopped his response and continued searching, eventually responding to the suspect's scent.

The newspapers followed the discussion in court: all of the evidence, including the line-up, was examined critically, and the suspect was acquitted twice. An important part of the discussion concerned the handler's prior knowledge of the position of the suspect's scent in the line-up. Although most people agreed that the evidence would have been stronger had the handler not known, they did not really seem aware of the possible extent of the consequences of this knowledge. For instance, while Major Feijlbrief, staff officer of the Dutch National Police Force and supervisor of the National Police Dogs service, supported the opinion of the commander of the Dutch National Tracking Dog School that it was better not to know the scent's position, he saw the court's hesitation to accept the results of the line-up as an attack on the integrity of the police dog handler who conducted it. For Major Feijlbrief, this was unacceptable.

Of course, it is possible for a dog to react to signals that the handler himself is unaware of. A slight catching of breath or a relaxation of muscles once the dog is paying attention to the "correct" scent—these can be made involuntarily, without the handler even realizing he's doing it. When a handler reacts in these way, especially if he does so regularly, his dog can start using these signals as a very reliable way to be rewarded. but insofar as these behaviors are involuntary, they of course have nothing to do with the integrity of the handler.

* This story is summarized from Eijk, "Heksenjacht op een zwerver" (Witch hunt for a bum).

The Importance of Working Single- and Double-Blind

We believe that dog handlers and trainers who work in scent identification or detection must approach human influence on dogs with the utmost seriousness, and ask: How can we prevent ourselves or other from cueing our dogs if dogs can pick up on and respond to such minimal, unconscious signals? The answer is obvious: Work single-blind or, better, double-blind, and do so as quickly as possible.

Line-ups, when performed carefully and under controlled conditions, are an ideal way to work double-blind with your dog. Such measures will enormously improve a dog's performance and ensure the results of your dog's work can be trusted. As we will see, in the context of suspect discrimination, failing to maintain a double-blind environment can have serious consequences not only on the quality of your evidence, but on the reputation of the use of dogs in scent identification as a whole. When it comes to detection, knowing how to set up a reliable double-blind line-up is important to training your dog to work in the real world—because after all, out there, double-blind is the only context there is!

We can divide different scent and odor line-up scenarios into five categories:

1. The handler places the target scent(s) or odor(s) himself, then performs the search with the dog.
2. The handler asks an assistant to place the target scent(s) or odor(s) according to the handler's instructions.
3. An assistant places the target scent(s) or odor(s) according to his own schema. The handler does not know this schema. When the handler is searching with his dog, the assistant is still present in the search area.
4. An assistant places the target scent(s) or odor(s) according to his own schema, then leaves the search area. The handler and dog are alone in the search area.
5. An assistant who is unknown to the dog places the target scent(s) or odor(s) according to his own schema, then leaves the search area. The handler and dog are alone in the search area.

In general, we call categories 1 and 2 "known" searches, as the position of the target smell is known to the handler. Category 3 searches are "single-blind": the handler does not know the position of the target smell, but others are present (e.g., the assistant) who *do* know its position, and this may still have an influence on the dog. Categories 4 and 5 are "double-blind," as no one present at the line-up knows the position of the target smell. In category 5, even the familiar scent of a known assistant is removed, lessening even further any possible human influence on the dog.

When we work double-blind, the "interface" of our search becomes clearer to outside observers, and our results become more reliable. This doesn't mean we can completely avoid false alerts or responses. Everyone makes mistakes. But if we all try to understand how and why the mistakes are made, we can use this information to our advantage by changing our systems to avoid these mistakes in the future. By paying attention to mistakes, we can make our line-ups and searches even better.

BUILDING CONFIDENCE

Starting a double-blind exercise can be quite nerve-racking. We have no clue where the target scents or odors are, and this lack of knowledge is uncomfortable—but it's also the point. Still, nervousness itself can have a direct impact on the performance of any dog, particularly if the dog is used to scanning the handler for information about hides and target scent. When a dog not only gains no information from the handler, but also senses the handler's discomfort, the dog will lose his confidence in the search.

Stick with it. After a few repetitions, trust and confidence is usually restored, and a very proud handler starts to become even prouder of his dog. The dog will notice this change in his handler. Calm and confidence will inspire much different work in a dog than nervousness and anxiety ever will.

THE 80% RULE

It is important to remember that no dog team will be 100% accurate all of the time. False indications (also called *alerts* or *responses*, depending on your training context) will happen. They can be either negative or positive. A false negative indication is when the dog gives us no alert or response despite the fact that there is a target smell in the search area. Essentially, it means the dog has missed its target. Conversely, a false positive indication is when the dog alerts or responds in an area where there is *no* target smell. It is important to understand these false indications and include them as part of the training program to better equip you next time.

A reliable scent identification or detection dog will have an 80% success rate. This is the success rate you should be training for. But what does that actually mean?

To measure your dog's success rate, you need to split your training into measurable chunks. We call these chunks *sessions* and *trials*. A session is a period of time or a specific number of trials during which we train. A trial is a single rehearsal of a specific training step or exercise. For instance, a basic "sit" training program might consist of 26 different sessions, each with 10 trials that get longer and more complex as the dog becomes more experienced and adept. A single training step may be trained across multiple sessions.

Some handlers just train a few trials per session, will skip training trials if the dog is doing well, and will move quickly onto new training steps. This won't give us a good idea of how successful the dog actually is at the task being trained. It won't give us good data. With only a handful of successes, it's hard to tell whether the dog knows what he's doing or is just lucky.

Figuring out whether your dog is achieving an 80% success rate is all about collecting good data. We like to split up our training sessions—especially the early ones that teach basic skills—into 10 trials of a single training step. It is important to complete all 10 trials in each session, even if the dog appears to be performing well. Later, as the dog progresses in its training and training sessions become longer, we can begin using fewer trials per session, but the initial 10-trial sessions play an important role. For one, they give the dog more repetitions, which helps with conditioning. They also make it easy to calculate your dog's success rate: if your dog gets it right eight times in a session, you're ready to move on to the next step.

Record your dog's performance on a simple datasheet like Table 0.1. You can also use your datasheet to record other aspects of your training session, such as environmental factors and equipment used. Over time, this information may help you to identify particular circumstances in which your dog struggles or excels, and allows you to adjust your training accordingly.

Our data shows us that the best results are achieved after an average of 40 to 50 total repetitions, or four to five 10-trial sessions per training step, with your dog achieving at least an 80% success rate in the last session. If you want to do an excellent job, then only allow yourself to move to the next step in training if your dog has

Table 0.1 Simple training session datasheet

Training venue:		
Training goal:		
Temperature:		
Environmental distractions:		

TRIAL	RESULT		
	Success	False +	False −
1			
2			
3			
4			
5			
6			
7			
8			
9			
10			

had an 80% success rate on a single step in at least two consecutive sessions. If the dog scores 80% in the first session but only 70% in the second session, the dog is not ready to move to the next training level.

What You'll Learn in This Book

The book is organized into two parts. In Part I, we deal with scent identification line-ups. The line-up has obvious value for training dogs in scent identification, but also has a long history of being used for the purposes of police suspect identification in more or less standardized ways and with more or less emphasis on working double-blind. The line-up procedure developed by the Dutch police is the only standardized, double-blind line-up procedure in the world that has been scientifically verified. For this reason, Part I focuses on this Dutch line-up procedure. Readers will learn about its historical development, how to correctly train search dogs in this line-up procedure, and how best to implement this procedure as a search dog handler.

Part II focuses on how line-ups can be used in the fascinating work of detection training. Unlike suspect identification work, line-ups are not typically used to structure the actual, professional work of a detection dog. Most professional detection dogs work in area and building searches to both discriminate among specific odors and pinpoint the exact location of an odor's strongest source. However, line-ups are still extremely useful for imprinting new odors on search dogs and for training correct alert techniques, which are both necessary to operational work. Line-ups are also used as the basic structure of odor recognition tests, which most dogs must pass to be certified in detection, and which are also used in sport contexts. Readers will learn the basics of line-up detection training using different types of reinforcement techniques. They will also learn the specifics of training for the ACT! Odor Recognition Test, designed by Simon Prins. Finally, readers will be introduced to scent wheel training (which, despite its name, is designed to train dogs in scent *and* odor work) as an alternative method of detection training that avoids some of the downfalls of the traditional line-up.

Throughout the book, you'll encounter vocabulary that is specific to K9 scent and odor work. In these lines of work as much as within the pages of this book, it's important that we're all in agreement as to exactly what these words mean. For this reason, we've also included a glossary of terms at the back of the book. We hope this helps you keep track of the concepts you learn here and to establish a standard way of communicating with your colleagues and clubmates.

By the end of the book, we hope that readers will not only feel confident in their ability to implement a high-quality, double-blind line-up training with their search dogs, but also to distinguish between the search techniques that are reliable, and those that are not.

Part I

Suspect Identification and
Scent Identification Line-ups

1

Introduction to Canine Suspect Identification and Scent Identification Line-ups

In a scent identification line-up, dogs are trained to match a scent deposited on an object to the same scent on deposited on a second object, or scent carrier—usually, a small steel tube or piece of neutral-smelling cloth. In a real-world policing situation, the scent object will be a *corpus delicti* (literally, the "body of the crime"): an object related to a crime that investigators are reasonably sure was touched by the perpetrator, such as a murder weapon. The line-up will contain the scent of a suspect under investigation, along with scents from other, unrelated people, called *foils*. The dog is used to try to determine whether the scent on the corpus delicti matches the suspect's scent in the line-up. Because these line-ups are all about identifying a suspect based on their individual scent, we also call them scent identification line-ups.

Can dogs really perform this kind of scent-matching with any reliability? The answer is yes, so long as the line-ups are carefully set up and performed. Understanding what makes a good line-up and how to train for it is the purpose of Part I of this book. In this first chapter, we'll take a closer look at human scent itself, and

Figure 1.1 A Dutch police dog searches a row of metal tubes scented with human scent.

how it must be handled and preserved to make line-ups possible. We'll also look at the traits that dogs and handlers must possess in order to meet and excel in the challenging requirements of scent identification work.

Can Dogs Recognize Me by My Scent?

Numerous studies have indicated that dogs are able to differentiate humans by their scent, and a number of studies have shown that canines are even able to match human scents from different parts of the body. Moreover, dogs have a proven ability to recognize and match a given scent from objects with a person who had previously touched them.[1] This is because dogs have incredible olfactory capacity, but it's also because every human being has their own particular human scent that stays constant over time.

The source of human scent is the body. Historically, it was thought that human scent comes from dead skin cells alone. In fact, according to the American Academy for Forensic Sciences Standards Board, human scent is made up of a combination of "volatile chemicals emitted from a live human."[2] Curran, Rabin, and Furton suggest that the human scent consists of three types of scents, emitted from three major sweat-related glands: the apocrine, eccrine, and sebaceous glands.[3] According to Vyplelová et al., human scent is also the result of a complex combination of factors including heredity, environment, experience, diet, and other lifestyle habits and genetic attributes.[4] All of this contributes to the fact that every human being has a unique scent, like a fingerprint, which they share with no one else.

Our particular scents are persistent and stable. While washing does minimize the amount of lipids on the skin, therefore minimizing the *amount* of scent we give off, it does not fundamentally alter our individual scent, and the weakening effect is short lived. Individual humans also tend to maintain a "signature scent" across time. Behavioral studies in humans have shown, for example, that siblings can recognize each other's recently deposited scent even after as much as a 30-month separation.[5]

Were these facts not true, a scent identification line-up would not be possible. First, were human scents not unique, there would be no point in trying to find a match at all. And second, the time period between a perpetrator depositing their scent on a corpus delicti and an investigatory scent identification line-up can be significant. If a person's scent did not remain stable, making a match would be impossible.

That being said, scents deposited on objects do change, at least in part, over time. Remember: scents are made up of volatile chemicals such as lipids secreted by the human body. Once these chemicals have been secreted, they begin to disperse and break down—this is what *volatile* means. The consequences of this volatility can be gleaned from a study of the chemical changes observed in fingerprint deposits. This study showed that the saturated fatty compounds in the fingerprint remain relatively stable over time. However, the unsaturated lipids (such as squalene and some of the fatty acids) diminished substantially in a 30-day period, especially during the first week. With time, these unsaturated lipids were replaced with saturated, low-molecular acids: the product of their breakdown. The older the sample, the more these saturated components dominated.[6]

It is reasonable to assume that a similar breakdown occurs in scent deposits. Indeed, this assumption is confirmed by the fact that most dogs find it more difficult to successfully perform a scent identification line-up with an old scent object or corpus delicti. One study conducted with Dutch and German scent identification dogs using old scent objects showed that the performance level dropped significantly between line-ups using fresh (0-day-old) objects and those using 2-week-old objects (which was the next time frame measured).[7] But this doesn't mean that such matches are impossible. In the same study, the dogs' performance, though diminished compared to the fresh scent object, remained the same whether they were using 2-week-old or 6-month-old objects. Remember: some lipid deposits *do* remain stable across time. In the case of scents, those produced by sebaceous glands appear to be the most stable.[8]

The difficulty of matches with older scents can be counterbalanced with proper training. Dogs need to be slowly introduced to older and older objects, beginning with freshly scented objects and increasing the age by hours, not days, until they can reliably work with week-old object. Once these are no longer a problem, dogs can manage much older objects with the same ease.

WORKING DOGS, SCENTS, AND CORPORA DELICTI

Just because human beings have unique scents doesn't mean a dog is guaranteed to make a perfect scent match every time. Just as we can use a fingerprint as an analogy for scent, so can we use fingerprint analysis as an analogy for scent identification line-ups. The success of a fingerprint analysis, as for that of a scent identification line-up, depends on the quality of the print or scent, the way it was retrieved, the material or object it was retrieved from, and how relevant that object actually is to a case.

There is one important difference between fingerprint analysis and scent identification line-ups: fingerprint analysis is done by a human being. A fingerprint expert first analyzes the quality of the fingerprint on an object. He can then say whether the quality of the fingerprint is sufficient to make reliable comparisons and to submit as evidence in an investigation. The fingerprint expert will simply not work with poor-quality fingerprints; he will limit his work to good starting material. Unfortunately, there is no similar method to measure or verify the quality of the scent left on an object. Dogs can tell us a lot, but they can't tell us that. From experiments, it is known that dogs can detect human scent on objects, even those that have been left outside for days and sometimes weeks.[9] However, just because a dog *can* do this does not mean that the quality of such a scent, or the fullness of the scent picture, is sufficient for the dog to be able to identify the person who left it.

With this in mind, selecting a corpus delicti from which to collect a scent sample must be done in an intelligent way. In general, objects that have been brought to the crime scene by the perpetrator are best. Objects found on the scene of the crime that have, with a reasonable degree of certainty, been touched by the perpetrator are also good. Wet or dirty objects, objects that several people have touched, or objects that have been lying outside for a couple of days are less desirable, but cannot be excluded, especially if they are significant to the case.

COLLECTING AND STORING SCENT TRACES IN A WORKING CONTEXT

Corpora delicti and scent traces must be collected carefully and systematically to avoid contaminating them with further scents or odors. Even if you are an amateur or hobby trainer and are unlikely to find yourself at a crime scene, it is still important for you to understand the basics of scent trace collection and storage in order to be successful in your training.

Here, we go over the protocols for scent trace collection developed by the Dutch police force. Different jurisdictions will have different protocols around the storage of evidence for scent work, so make sure you know the protocols where you work.

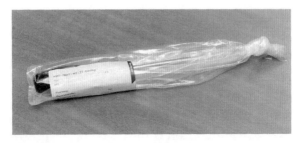

Figure 1.2 A screwdriver collected at a crime scene, packaged and labeled for evidence storage.

The first person at a crime scene must keep in mind that there are likely scent traces present that can be used for scent identification line-ups, and must take all necessary precautions to identify these and ensure they are not contaminated or destroyed. Consider, for example, a crime scene in which a window has been forced open and a crowbar is lying underneath it. The officer on scene might make the reasonable assumption that the perpetrator used the crowbar to open the window. If the perpetrator did indeed use it, and especially if they brought the crowbar with them to the scene, it will contain this person's scent. Knowing this, the officer should ensure that no one touches the object, at least until a scent trace can be collected. (Note that there may be more than one relevant object, all of which should be treated in the same way.)

The scent evidence must then be collected and preserved. As early as in 1911, Friedo Schmidt wrote about the way articles found at a crime scene should be saved and stored:

> By no means should the article be left at the scene or be taken in hand by the criminal investigator. This must be common knowledge to every man working at the crime scene. The article must also not be wrapped in paper or packed in a wooden or cardboard box because before long it will take the odor of the strange material.
>
> I suggest glass containers as the best means of storage. Glass is an inert material. Substances like sweat, blood, etc. incur no changes in contact with glass. Every separate

article, as well as size allows, must be put in an appropriately sized, wide-necked sealable glass-receptacle equipped with a glass-stopper. Such containers have the advantage of transparency, so that the article, for instance a handkerchief, can easily pass from hand to hand and important details, such as a monogram, can also be observed whilst in the receptacle.[10]

By and large, Schmidt's principles still apply today, though nowadays it is common to use plastic as well. If the identified objects are relatively small, they may be preserved as a whole. This can be done by putting them in a thick plastic bag, expelling as much air as possible out of the bag, and sealing it. It may also, as Schmidt prescribes, be placed in a sterile glass jar with a twist-off top.

If the object is big and unwieldy, if it cannot be removed (e.g., a seat in a car), or if it needs to be used for other purposes in the investigation, a scent sample can be made. A scent sample is made by placing a piece of cotton absorber over the object, covering it (usually with aluminum foil) to avoid contamination, and pressing or weighing it down onto the object to maximize contact. After 30 minutes, the scent absorber is removed and carefully stored as above.

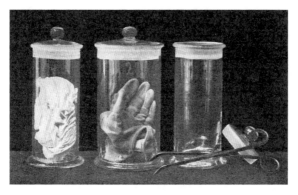

Figure 1.3 Objects sealed to prevent loss of scent for later investigation, as suggested by Friedo Schmidt in 1911.

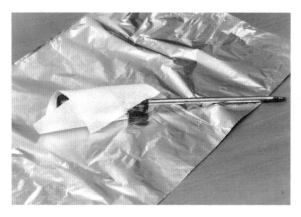

Figure 1.4 Taking a scent sample from an object collected at a crime scene.

Figure 1.5 A piece of evidence found at a crime scene.

Collected scent traces should be stored in dark, temperature-controlled rooms. Sunlight is especially detrimental to scent, so avoid it as much as possible. It is also highly recommended to limit access to this room and implement a proper registration system showing incoming and outgoing articles.

A special note must be made here. With the advance of science, objects that are collected at a crime scene are examined in many different ways. The sequence of these examinations, and their potential to destroy evidence that may be used in a different examination process, has become a point of interest among forensics experts. For example, rubbing an object with a cotton absorber for scent sample collection will certainly destroy any fingerprints present. If fingerprints are to be collected, it is therefore better not to rub the object, but to drape the cotton absorber loosely over it.

Special precautions must also be taken if a piece of evidence is being used for both DNA analysis and scent identification. Never place evidence that may contain DNA in plastic bag or glass container because these retain moisture, which will damage the DNA sample. Evidence that may contain DNA must, exceptionally, be secured in paper bags or envelopes, then transported and stored in dry, temperature-controlled environments.

The Right Stuff for the Job

Scent identification training will only be successful with the right ingredients. This is true of correctly collected scent traces, as we just discussed; of carefully set-up line-ups, as we will discuss in Chapter 4; and of well-selected and -paired dogs, handlers, and teams, which we will discuss here. It's obvious to most people that we must look carefully at the characteristics of the dog we want to train to make sure it is up to the task. But it is equally important to consider the characteristics of the handler who will be training the dog, and the kind of team the handler and his dog make together. Scent identification line-ups, though not physically strenuous, are perhaps the most mentally challenging kind of search dog work. They therefore requires a calm, patient, and mature attitude on the parts of both the dog and its handler, as well as a strong and trusting working relationship between them.

PHYSICAL QUALITIES OF DOG AND HANDLER

Even though performing scent identification line-ups is not particularly physically challenging, it is still very necessary to have a healthy dog. Many kinds of illnesses and medication affect the

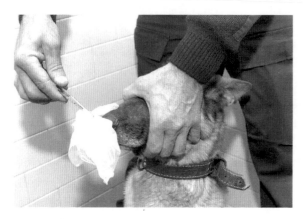

Figure 1.6 A handler having his dog smell the piece of evidence found at a crime scene.

canine nose. Training the dog while his sense of smell is less than optimal will lead to all kinds of unnecessary and stressful situations that will be detrimental to training and may lead to training failure.

A dog who is a good candidate for scent training will:

- Be completely healthy
- Move easily
- Have a strong sense of smell
- Have a healthy mouth (incomplete teeth are not a problem, but we have found that bad breath as a result of plaque interferes with olfaction)

The handler will not find scent identification line-ups overly physically taxing, though it does require frequent bending over, squatting, and kneeling. These movements must not be challenging for the handler.

MENTAL QUALITIES OF DOG AND HANDLER

While physical health is very important to scent identification work, mental health and acuity is arguably the most important trait to look for in a dog. Again, among the traditional searching dog activities, scent identification demands the most from dog and handler in terms of cognitive ability—even more than

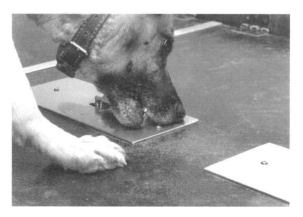

Figure 1.7 A dog responds to a scent tube in a scent identification line-up.

detection. In the latter, a dog must memorize a number of specifically trained target smells and then track them down when they appear. Scent identification line-ups involve remembering a new, never-before-smelled scent and matching it to samples. What's more, they involve discriminating between multiple human scents that, though all unique, may nonetheless be quite similar to one another. Scent identification therefore requires dogs and handlers of particular mental strength.

A dog who is a good candidate for scent identification training will:

- Be self-confident and stable, not nervous or afraid
- Be lively and interested
- Be willing to work, and continue the be willing even when there is no immediate reward
- Be able to quickly learn to respond to a cue
- Have a good search drive and a natural ability to use its nose to find objects
- Not be too prey driven: if the dog defends his reward too strongly, he will be too focused on the reward itself, which will prevent it from searching well
- Have a good retrieving drive: by bringing his reward—for instance, the scent tube from the line-up—to the handler, the dog shares it with the handler and this is good for the team

- Be able to cope with mistakes: if verbally corrected, the dog should remain composed and willing to work with high search and retrieval drives

Dogs without these qualities—and particularly dogs that cannot quickly cope with making mistakes and being corrected—are difficult to work with in scent identification line-ups.

Although training for scent identification can begin before puberty, the mental qualities necessary for this work are only found in mature dogs. We have not found that starting early with scent-specific training significantly shortens the training time or increases the final performance level. However, you can begin to prepare a young dog for scent identification by providing opportunities for good socialization, training general obedience, and stimulating search and retrieval drives through games (though you should avoid making a dog too possessive of any object that might be used in a line-up). Care should be taken to ensure that the dog learns to search with its nose. The active use of the nose enhances the development of the dog's olfactory abilities, ensuring a good starting-point for scent training.

It's also important to know that some of the necessary mental characteristics will only become apparent, or may even develop, during training. You can try to test willingness to work, for example, beforehand, but the dog will have to prove its willingness by consistently and enthusiastically performing scent identifications. At the end of the day, scent identification line-ups are quite routine with little variety; this may ultimately make a difference to the dog. The ability to cope with mistakes in the line-up is another characteristic that can't be tested beforehand, and must be carefully attended to in training.

Handlers must also have a high level of intelligence and mental toughness. They must be calm in character and not easily agitated by their dog's behavior. A good handler working in suspect identification must have a strong and proven ability to interpret the behaviors and alert signals of different dogs quickly and correctly. She must have a lot of patience, be willing to review her own training critically, and not be afraid to go back a step in training if needed (and this is regularly needed!). She must accept that a good scent identification dog will not pay very much attention to her, which is quite different from normal obedience work.

The handler must also be very aware of the possible pitfalls of scent identification work, and particularly of handler influence. She must realize that the dog is the only one who can smell well enough to solve the problem, and must therefore never try to force the dog into making a choice in the line-up. She must adapt her training to help the dog into understand what she expects him to do—to make a scent identification with its nose—and avoid teaching the dog to rely on her. In short, she must be an intelligent and sensitive trainer who stays one step ahead of her dog at all times in training—but not when it comes to actually making the line-up identification. So, if you want to start working in K9 scent identification, look at yourself critically. Are you truly someone like this?

THE DOG-AND-HANDLER TEAM

An inadequate handler can ruin a potentially good dog. A good handler can go quite a long way with a not-so-good dog. A handler and dog who don't get along are unlikely to resolve their issues. In any case, a poor match will make it impossible for a team to achieve the high standard necessary for operational work. If things are not going well, stop. Any stress between the handler and the dog will negatively affect your performance in a scent identification line-up.

When assessing the quality of a team, begin with the handler. It is very important that the handler likes the dog he is paired with, and that he feels no tension with the dog. Then look at the team. They should have a relaxed relationship both in and outside

Figure 1.8 The handler releases the tube for the dog to retrieve in a training session. On the wall, the whiteboard registers the location of the scents on the platform. The information on the whiteboard may only be visible in a training situation that is not double-blind. In an actual investigation, this information must be erased from the board.

Figure 1.9 A dog is rewarded with the scent tube it has responded to.

of training. Any activities that the team does together outside of training should suit both the dog and the handler, and should consistently improve their relationship.

You should, by now, have a better sense of what scent is, how it makes a scent identification line-up possible, and how to collect that all-important scent trace. You should also understand *who* should perform scent identification work. In the next chapter, we'll look in more detail at the concept of the scent identification line-up itself, and how it has developed over time to ultimately produce a reliable, scientifically proven methodology.

2

The Early History of Canine Suspect Identification in Europe

The scent identification line-up has been widely used in policing around the world for more than 100 years, and its usefulness as a forensic tool for suspect identification is recognized in many countries.[1] But the protocols around how these line-ups are performed differ from jurisdiction to jurisdiction, and sometimes even within jurisdictions. These differences can create perceived and actual unreliability in line-up results.[2]

This chapter tells the story of early German and Dutch use of dogs in suspect identification, as this history is important to the development of the standard Dutch scent identification line-up procedure—the only scientifically developed scent line-up in the world (the history of which we go through in detail in Chapter 3).

Scent Identification Line-ups in Germany

One cannot give a history of canine scent identification in Europe without first mentioning Inspector Bussenius. Bussenius lived and worked in Braunschweig, Germany, at the beginning of the twentieth century. He championed the use of police dogs as investigative tools and was a very good police dog trainer himself. By using

Figure 2.1 A German policeman with his dog, about 1910.

his dogs in the city of Braunschweig, he provided the authorities with important examples of the usefulness of dogs' olfactory abilities as forensic, investigative tools. Bussenius's successful use of his German Shepherd dog Harras von der Polizei in a particular murder case near Braunschweig in 1903 showed Germany, and the world, the value of a dog in the investigation of homicide cases. This case—which we call the Duwe murder after the accused farmhand at its center—is seen as a turning point in the history of the police dog.

Dr. Friedo Schmidt summarizes the Duwe case:

An 11-year-old girl was killed at the Hagenhof farm in the German village of Königslutter near Braunschweig on

June 3, 1903. The forensic research team did not come up
with results although one of the farmhands was suspected.
After days of continuous but fruitless investigation, the
public prosecutor asked Inspector Bussenius from Braunschweig to try to find the murderer with his German
Shepherd dog Harras von der Polizei. After their arrival
at the Hagenhof farm—four days after the homicide—all
twelve employees of the farm were placed in a line in the
yard. After that, Harras was brought to the crime scene,
where Inspector Bussenius commanded him to sniff the
bloodstains and the surrounding area. The dog immediately
picked up the track. First he briefly scanned one of the
forensic investigators who had visited the crime scene earlier. Before long, the dog left him and continued tracking.
The dog then sniffed each person standing in the line, one
after the other. Suddenly, when he reached the eighth position in line, Harras hurled himself at the man who cried out
loudly in protest. The accused man was the suspected farmhand Duwe. The test was repeated two times. Each time,
the people in the line changed positions, but the result was
always the same: Harras hurling himself furiously at Duwe,
and not paying attention to the other persons. After that,
Duwe was arrested. In the beginning, Duwe tried to deny
the murder, but soon he made a full confession. Duwe was
condemned to death.

A week later, a dog enthusiast sent one Reichsmark to
the Braunschweig police department to buy a reward of
beef steak for Harras.[3]

After the initial success of Harras and Inspector Bussenius, it
was only a short time before other dogs and their handlers began
working homicide cases and getting results. Beginning in October
1909, the *Verein für deutsche Schäferhunde* (German Shepherd Dog
Society, or SV) offered a 25-Mark reward to every dog handler
who successfully solved a homicide case using a German Shepherd dog. In a period of 18 months, the SV paid this cash prize

Figure 2.2 The German police reports of the early twentieth century contain a lot of unbelievable tracking results in finding the houses of criminals. In many cases, the dog was led by its handler to the home of a suspect.

18 times. In 1911, Schmidt reacted to the rapidly increasing use of dogs in German policing:

> One case after the other was solved, so that we can now look back upon a considerable number of murder cases successfully settled by the work of German Shepherd dogs. This success cannot only be attributed to the perfect aptitude of the dogs, but certainly also to our bold dog handlers. This work has a special value, not only providing important information about the crime case itself, but also for the authorities to assess the value of the dog in criminal investigation, just as these successes are helpful in convincing the public of the value of the police dog.[4]

UNBELIEVABLE RESULTS

It is interesting to read the German reports of the early 1900s, some of which involve amazing—even unbelievable—results. Schmidt documents some of these incredible cases, some of which involved dogs not only following a track, but also performing suspect identification.

In one 1908 case involving the murder of a young boy, a K9 team in the town of Giessen in Germany—Greif von Wetzlar and his handler Sergeant Jacob—performed a combination of tracking and scent identification that ultimately led to the conviction of the suspected murder, a cobbler's apprentice named Reif. As Schmidt tells it, although more than 72 hours had passed since the murder, and despite inclement weather, Jacob and Greif began performing a 3.5-km track based on the scents found on the murdered boy's clothes. This initial track was inconclusive and had to be stopped when the sun began to set. The next day, at the order of a public prosecutor, Jacob and Greif tried the track again, this time placing several people along the track including the suspect, Reif. As Schmidt reports, "The dog sniffed briefly at first two persons, but when he came to the third person, the suspect Reif, he sniffed him, barked, then lunged at Reif's chest so violently that they could hardly bring Greif away from Reif. After some time, Reif confessed to the murder."[5] Sergeant Jacob was the first officer to receive the SV cash reward in 1909 for his work in another case.

Schmidt also describes a 1909 murder case in which two policemen and their German Shepherds Prinz von Mühlenberg and Bolko von Klostermansfeld performed a series of tracks and scent identifications that ultimately led to an arrest in the murder of a young girl on the Dallmin estate near Westpriegnitz, Germany. By the time the officers arrived, officers from Havelberg had already tried to pick up a track with their patrol dog—an Airedale Terrier—with no results. It was November, and snowing. Still, Prinz and his handler, Patrolman Frank, tried to pick up a track as the light faded. Prinz was able to follow the track into the woods to a coach house on the property before he lost it in the snow. It was enough, however, for officers to conclude that the culprit must be someone who resided on the estate. Two suspects were taken into custody: a laborer with a scratched-up face and the gardener's assistant, Pöhling, who investigators suspected, although the murdered girl's father and the magistrate assigned to the case both presumed him to be innocent. Pöhling was placed in a line-up among a number of other servants from the estate. Frank gave Prinz a scent from the bottom front of the girl's skirt—an area he believe to carry the scent of the perpetrator. As Prinz approached the line-up, he showed no reaction until he came to Pöhling, at which point he started barking and looking back and forth between Pöhling and his handler, Frank. Prinz then bit Pöhling on the leg. In his book, Schmidt interprets this bite as the result of Prinz "fear[ing] his signal could be misunderstood."[6] Pöhling eventually made a detailed confession, and recounted how he had killed the child with a knife, which he then threw into the woods. The next day, two days after the murder, the dog Bolko took the scent from Pöhling's hands and soon found the knife. Prinz's handler, Patrolman Frank from the village of Schöneberg, was the second person to receive the SV reward.

Miraculous stories like these were common in police dog literature of the early-1900s. Most of the search dog trainers, together with the journalists writing the accounts, spoke in exaggerated terms about the results of these dogs. The work of police dogs was fully and often uncritically trusted among police and in judicial circles, and the clues provided by the dogs were accepted as solid evidence. The more cases were "solved" in this way, the greater people's faith in a dog's ability to straightforwardly point out the guilty person.

Based on what we know today, these unbelievable stories are just that—they cannot be believed. Little thought seems to have been given at the time to the quality of scent traces used. Dogs trained to follow tracks were also used in scent identification tasks—something we now understand to be a different skill set that requires specific training. The lack of standardized protocols makes it more than likely that many of these results were influenced by the handler and their beliefs about the "most likely" suspect and the dogs' crime-solving capacity. This likely led to many excesses in criminal investigations and punishment.

By the beginning of the First World War, police dog handlers began looking more critically at police dog work and scent evidence, and began to realize its limitations and pitfalls. The value of dogs' capacity to identify people based on their scent, however, remained evident.

Moving Toward Precision

During the First World War, scent identification in the Netherlands was led by the forensics expert Dr. C. J. van Ledden Hulsebosch from Amsterdam. He traveled all over the Netherlands with Officer Jacob Water and his dog Albert, a fawn, longhaired Belgian Shepherd, following tracks and identifying suspects.

While the work Water and van Ledden Hulsebosch did with Albert does not exactly resemble the scent line-ups we are familiar with in the Netherlands today, compared to the earlier line-ups performed in Germany, it does illustrate a move toward greater precision and care in the way scent tracking and identification was carried out, as well as more critical interpretation of the results. Ultimately, van Ledden Hulsebosch's investigative design and Water's and Albert's performances formed the foundation of later developments in police scent identification line-ups and the use of search dogs more generally.

ALBERT'S INVESTIGATIONS

Albert, Water, and van Ledden Hulsebosch were called in to investigate the murder of the director of a milk factory whose throat was cut with a razor.[7] A cap and a razor were found in the factory near the spot where the man was killed. When first asked for assistance, Albert was given scent from the razor and later on from the cap. He tracked through the factory then outside to a tree where the murderer had probably mounted a bicycle and left the scene.

In the meantime, it was rumored that a man who was known to the police had been seen in the vicinity of the factory. Almost three weeks later, this man was arrested. However, he denied being the murderer. Again, Albert was asked for help. The suspect was placed in a circle together with other people. After sniffing at the razor, the dog pointed out the suspect without hesitation. This man continued to deny involvement with the murder.

A second test was then carried out. The caps of all those present were spread out on the ground along with the cap found in the factory. Albert sniffed at the suspect then went to the pile of caps. Soon he picked out a cap, but this was not the one found in the factory. After searching again, Albert brought the cap found in the factory to his handler. The first cap belonged to the suspect: he was wearing it when he was arrested. Officer Water concluded that since this cap contained the strongest scent of the suspect, it was picked out by the dog first.

In January 1918, Albert and Bob, Amsterdam's first police dog, were called in to solve another murder case, this time of a farmer from the area around Breezand in the Netherlands. Two suspects

Figure 2.3 Albert performing a scent identification line-up on caps in the case of the murdered director. Top left: The arrest. Right: Mr. Van Ledden Hulsebosch giving police dog Albert scent from the found razor.

were identified based on fingerprints and other clues. One of these suspects confessed to the crime, saying that he and the other suspect removed their shoes before climbing through a small window in a cowshed. The other suspect accidentally stepped into some manure in the shed. After the murder, he stepped back into his shoe with the soiled sock. Van Ledden Hulsebosch immediately wanted to examine the second man's shoes. This man, thinking quickly, said that he had visited the cattle market and had gotten manure on his sock there. This led van Ledden Hulsebosch to an idea: use the dogs to discriminate between the odors of manure from different cattle sheds.

Officer Water writes:

> To our nose, the manure of one cow smells much the same as the other so the dung would not necessarily have to be incriminating. But Mr. Van Ledden Hulsebosch felt differently. He thought dogs could distinguish manure from different cowsheds. Therefore, he asked the gendarme from Breezand to bring him cow manure from twelve different cowsheds including that where the murder had taken place, in twelve well-cleaned jam jars. The jam jars were numbered and a list was compiled of the owners of the cowsheds.
>
> Now Mr. Van Ledden Hulsebosch took 72 equal pieces of paper and divided them into six series, each numbered from 1 to 12 according to the numbers on the jam jars. Manure was spread on the numbered papers then these were distributed throughout the courtyard of the police headquarters between shrubs and in all possible and impossible places…Mr. Van Ledden Hulsebosch first wanted to test whether the dogs were able to find dung from a particular shed through "sorting." To do this, I took a piece of paper with manure, let the dogs smell it, and commanded them to "search." Immediately the dogs started searching around and soon they found all the papers with the same number. To exclude all coincidence, the test was repeated several times with other manure papers, all with the same result.

As this experiment proved that the dogs could indeed discriminate between the manure from the different cowsheds, they were presented the left shoe to take scent. The dogs hesitated and stood still. Apparently they did not recognize the scent and they sniffed around listlessly. Then they were presented the right shoe, which as mentioned before had been stained with manure. Immediately their manner changed. They started wagging their tails and started searching. Very soon all the pieces of paper with the number of the jam jar containing the manure out of the cowshed where the murder had taken place were laid out before me. And as if he had wanted a crowning glory on his work, Albert brought the whole jam jar a few seconds later.[8]

Figure 2.4 Albert, the fawn, longhaired Belgian Shepherd of Police Officer Jacob Water, traveled during the First World War all over the Netherlands to follow tracks and identify suspects.

This case does not deal with dogs using human scent. However, it does show the use of a clever and systematic odor-discrimination procedure, and illustrates the capacity of dogs to clearly discriminate very similar odors from one another—a skill that is vital for scent identification.

INVESTIGATING ALBERT

Continuing the more critical stance toward police dog work in the early to mid-twentieth century, Prof. Dr. F. J. J. Buytendijk decided to examined Albert's scenting ability. He placed six people in a line-up. Each person took a pebble into his hand and, when signaled to do so, all threw their pebbles onto an already pebble-strewn path. Buytendijk then allowed Albert to sniff the hands of the first individual, and Officer Water commanded him to search. Albert searched the path, sniffing intently at each of the pebbles thrown onto the path, until he reached the first individual's pebble and retrieved it.

In his 1932 book on canine psychology, Buytendijk writes: "It was interesting to observe how the dog's behavior changed the moment he discovered the 'correct' pebble. While quietly searching from one spot to the other, all at once his ears stood on end and with fast movements of nose and mouth he isolated the pebble from the area then quickly retrieved it. The dog behaved in a totally different manner when he, either through the influence of his handler or other distractions, picked up a wrong pebble. In these cases, the dog reacted in an uncertain, almost shy manner."*

* Buytendijk, *De psychologie van den hond* (The psychology of the dog), 85. Our
  translation.

The Dutch National Tracking Dog School

Albert's achievements contributed to the establishment of the *Rijksspeurhondenschool*, the Dutch National Tracking Dog School for training police tracker dogs, in 1919. It was the first of its kind in the Netherlands. In later years, a number of municipal police forces set up their own tracking dog programs. The police forces in Rotterdam, Eindhoven, and Zaanstad each had their own dogs, trained by their own people, according to their own requirements. This created a rivalry between the municipal forces and the Dutch National Tracking Dog School that only ended in 1991, when official examination regulations were instated that applied to all Dutch police dogs and handlers. These regulations were the first in the world to mandate how scent identification line-ups should be conducted in forensic practice.

The 1991 regulations ultimately unified the national and municipal police forces in the Netherlands. In the new structure, the police canine unit became part of the Netherlands National Police Agency, which became responsible for training and certifying all Dutch police search dogs. In May 1996, the canine unit moved to a new building in Nunspeet, where it remains today. The space in this new complex allowed the unit to dedicate rooms specifically to scent identification line-ups.

Changes in the line-up protocols used by the tracking school 1920s illustrate changing views and insights over time. In 1997, new regulations were published for the Dutch search dog examination. The manner in which scent identification line-ups were to be conducted in forensic practice also changed, in accordance with

Figure 2.5 The Dutch National Tracking Dog School, founded 1919.

scientific developments. The 1997 line-up protocol—the result of history, experience, and scientific research within the Dutch National Tracking Dog School—remains the best-established protocol to date. The different phases in the development of this protocol are discussed in the next chapter.

The Development of a Standard Scent Identification Line-up

There is only one scent identification line-up procedure worldwide that has been scientifically developed to deliver, when performed carefully and correctly, reliable results to be used as evidence in court. This protocol was developed by the Netherlands National Police Agency (KLPD), and is still integral to the search dog program of the Royal Dutch Police Dog Association (KNPV). While KNPV training programs are not officially available outside the Netherlands, they are considered by many to be the gold standard in police dog training, including in the area of scent detection. The Dutch scent identification line-up protocol has even been adopted by the FBI in the United States.[1] For these reasons (along with the fact that we, your authors, are ourselves Dutch!), we focus on the KNPV scent identification line-up, its history, and its correct procedure in this chapter, and throughout Part I of this book.[2] Whether or not this is the procedure you use in your work or at your club, we believe that it is important for everyone who works in scent identification to know about the Dutch line-up procedure. It is equally important to understand what can go, and has gone, wrong in the implementation of scent line-up protocols in order to avoid these mistakes in the future.

Table 3.1 summarizes how Dutch scent identification line-ups developed over the last century at the KLPD's Dutch National Tracking Dog School. Each phase in this history is discussed in greater detail below.

1920s and 1930s: Person Line-ups

In the 1920s and 1930s, scent identification line-ups consisted of an actual line-up of people, like those described in some of the

Table 3.1 Summary of scent line-up protocols over the years

YEARS	LINE-UP DESIGN	TEST DESIGN	HANDLER KNOWLEDGE OF SCENT POSITION
1920s–1930s	1 row, 6 people	Choice repeated 2–3 times against different line-up sequences	Yes
1940s	1 row, any number of different objects scented by different people	Choice repeated 1–2 times on the same objects	Yes
1950s	1 row, any number of identical bunches of keys scented by different people	Choice repeated several times	Yes
1960s	1 row, 6–7 aluminum tubes scented by 3 foils and 1 suspect	Choice repeated several times, new tube of suspect scent used in the line-up each trial	Yes/No
1970s	1 row, 6–7 stainless-steel tubes scented by 3 foils and 1 suspect	Choice repeated several times, new tube of suspect scent used in the line-up each trial	Yes/No
1980s	2 × 6: 2 rows with the same 6 scents in different arrangements	Suspect scent occurs once in each row, dog searches each row once	No
1990s	12-scents: 12 different scents arranged in 2 rows of 6	1 row with suspect scent, 1 row without suspect scent, dog searches each row once	No
	4 × 6: 4 rows of 6 scents, with 2 rows containing 1 suspect scent each, and 2 rows containing only foil scents	Dog searches each row once	No
1997	Check-first: 2 rows of the same 7 scents; both rows include 1 control scent and 1 suspect scent	Dog searches each row once using a control scent, then searches each row once using a corpus delicti	No

stories in Chapter 2. In this type of line-up, the handler knew beforehand who the suspect was. The suspect was made to stand in a row together with a number of other people who, to the best of the investigators' knowledge, were not associated with the crime. (These people were called *foils*; the same term is used today to describe scent carriers that carry non-suspect and non-target scents.) Usually, a line-up would consist of about six people.

The object that contained the scent of the perpetrator, also called the corpus delicti, was kept in a preserving-bottle. The handler would let his dog smell the corpus delicti, then the dog would compare this scent with those of the people in the row. The dog would indicate a match, often by barking at that person. The line-up would then be repeated; the dog had to make the same choice two or three times for it to be recorded as a match.

An obvious drawback of the line-up of people is that the suspect, simply by being frightened of being a suspect, could react in a way that would influence the dog's choice. In fact, the nerves of anyone in the line-up could do this. The dog could simply be

Figure 3.1 A scent identification line-up of people. This is a still image from the 1948 film *Pech gehad* (Bad luck). In the film, the guilty man behaves nervously in the line-up while the others stare solidly ahead.

choosing someone based on their behavior rather than based on their scent—a risk confirmed by Professor Buytendijk, who commented in 1932 on the danger of "let[ting] a dog choose a person from a line-up of men based on the scent of an object, even when the handler doesn't know the test and doesn't suspect anyone, because there always will be a good chance that the dog would react to the slightest movement of one of the men in line."[3] In attempts to mitigate this effect, later variants of the person line-up had the suspect and foils stand behind closed blinds to prevent direct contact with the dog. Later still, fans were placed behind the people to blow the scent of each person straight through the blinds.

1940s: Object Line-ups

In the 1940s, people were replaced by scent-carrying objects. In this type of line-up, a number of foils were asked to put something

Figure 3.2 A scent identification line-up of people, ca. 1970. The people stand behind a blind to prevent direct contact with the dog. This method was used by Rotterdam police.

Figure 3.3 A scent identification line-up of worn shoes, ca. 1950.

that belonged to them in a row on the ground. An object that belonged to the suspect was added to this row. The handler performing these line-ups would know which object belonged to the suspect.

It is not known whether each foil object came from a different person, whether some objects came from the same people, or whether there was a standard procedure around this. The corpus delicti was still kept in the preserving-bottle. The handler would let his dog smell the corpus delicti, then send the dog to the line-up of objects to retrieve the object with the matching human scent. If this object belonged to the suspect, it would be replaced in the row (in another position) and the dog would be asked to repeat his choice a second or third time.

OBJECTS AND OBJECTIVITY

"Once I saw a scent identification test that obviously succeeded but which was absolutely incorrectly performed," Professor Buytendijk wrote in 1932.

According to Buytendijk, investigators wanted to know if a coat found at a crime scene (coat *A*) belonged to a particular suspect. The investigators set up an object line-up of six coats—five coats that belonged to officers and coat *A* from the crime scene. The investigators had a police dog take a scent directly from the suspect, then search the coats. The dog retrieved coat A.

"Such a test doesn't prove anything," Buytendijk writes. "Coat A would of course have a totally different scent profile than the coats belonging to the officers. Imagine that the scents were visible. In this case the dog would see five gray coats and a single red one so there would be a good chance that the dog would retrieve the one that was different than the others since it stood out. Only if all objects belonged to the same group of scent, and were optically identical in measurement and form, could there be a chance of obtaining reliable results."

As Buytendijk gravely instructs his readers, "May the report be a warning for ensuring the objective use of the police dog."*

* Buytendijk, *De psychologie van den hond* (The psychology of the dog), 87. Our translation.

1950s: Same-Object Line-ups

It gradually became clear that line-ups of mixed objects were not very objective. Dogs, like people, have preferences and, when it comes to line-ups, may easily prefer retrieving one type of object over others. This may be because they simply *like* retrieving a particular object—a stick, for example—or because one object differs drastically from the rest, making it stand out to the dog. In the 1950s, it therefore became standard practice to perform line-ups of objects, or scent carriers, in which all of the objects were the same. Bunches of keys were chosen as standard objects, since dogs had ample experience with them. The objects used in earlier object line-ups had often been keys.

At the Dutch National Tracking Dog School in the 1950s, identical bunches of keys were cleaned in boiling water and handed out to a number of people, including the suspect. The suspect and foils held the keys in their hands, with their hands in their pockets. The various sets of keys, now carrying different scents, were then placed in paper envelopes or preserving bottles until the actual scent identification line-up was performed. As in earlier years, the handler knew the position of the suspect's keys. The dog was given the scent of the corpus delicti and had to retrieve the matching bunch of keys a number of times, with the line-up being reset between trials. The Rotterdam police in these years used a similar line-up method using articles of clothing rather than bunches of keys.

1960s: Aluminum Tube Line-ups

Further changes in scent line-up procedures were made during the 1960s. Instead of the classic glass container, the corpus delicti was now preserved in modern plastic. Key bunches were replaced with small, uniform aluminum tubes, usually engraved with a number used to identify which tube belonged to which person. The suspect and foils held the tubes in their hands, and placed their hands in their pockets. For these line-ups, three non-suspects were given two tubes each, while the suspect was asked to hold three or four tubes. If a suspect was unwilling to hold the tubes in his hand, the tubes were scented in the armpits of his jacket. (For the Rotterdam police, the jacket method was the standard method used to obtain the scent of both the suspect and the foils.) The tubes were not used "warm"—that is, immediately after they were scented—but stored until the line-up was held.

The line-up was composed of six or seven tubes placed on a sorting board. After smelling the corpus delicti, the dog was asked to choose a tube. This process was repeated, mixing up the order of the scents using a fresh suspect tube each time, until no suspect tubes remained. (The same foil tubes were used in each line-up). The handler usually knew the position of the suspect's tube, but a number of them preferred not to know, already suspecting that their knowledge risked inadvertently influencing the dog.

The official scent identification line-up examination, which was carried out for the first time in the 1960s and overseen by the commander of the Dutch National Tracking Dog School, was comparable to the line-up procedure just described, except that all tubes were scented by being held in the hand, then used warm in the line-up. The corpus delicti (or, rather, the target-scent object, as the examination did not involve evidence from an actual crime scene) was also warm, being handed directly by the "suspect" to the handler.

1970s: Stainless-Steel Tube Line-ups

The 1970s scent identification line-up method was largely the same as in 1960s, with two key differences. First, the tubes were now scented in suspects' and foils' hands all across the Netherlands, and the jacket method was no longer used. Second, the aluminum tubes, which were soft and easily damaged by the dogs, were replaced by round, oval, or square stainless-steel tubes. These types of tubes are still used today.

When these tubes were originally introduced, no standards were in place around how to clean them after use to remove residual scents. The most common method was to let them boil dry in a pot on a stove, although some handlers used to simply leave the tubes in the sun for a while or put them on top of a radiator. Nowadays, the tubes are either sterilized in a stove or washed with soap in a dishwasher and then boiled in clean water.

1980s: Scent-Collection Cloths and the Two-by-Six Line-up

The 1980s saw innovations both in scent-collection methods and line-up procedures. Some of these innovations were spurred on by increasing pressure from the courts to provide better and more reliable scent identification evidence after several high-profile cases (including the "fitting-room murder," described in this chapter) brought methodological weaknesses and their real-world consequences into the public eye.

The 1980s also saw changes in the structure of K9 work in the Dutch police force. The KLPD moved tracking dog handlers from the criminal investigation department to the forensic department. This restructuring allowed for a new evaluation of the then current scent identification line-up procedures by those well versed in other forensic procedures. Together, KLPD forensic experts and K9 handlers developed a new forensic scent identification procedure, introduced in 1989. The Rotterdam and Zaanstad municipal police forces conformed to this standard procedure, nicknamed the two-by-six line-up.

SCENT-COLLECTION CLOTHS

Scent-collection cloths made their entry onto the scene in the 1980s. Using scent-collection cloths meant that scent could be collected directly from a corpus delicti (which could then be passed on for further forensic examination) and from otherwise unlikely places, such as the steering wheel or the seat of a car.

Originally, sterilized gauze pads were used as scent cloths. After some experimentation, however, Dutch police found that *Engels pluksel* (English cotton, a kind of cotton bandaging) worked best, and this became the standard. The Rotterdam police processed this material before use: fats were extracted, the cloths were dried, and each cloth was vacuum-packed separately in plastic.

THE TWO-BY-SIX LINE-UP

Two-by-six line-ups could contain up to two suspects along with four or five foils, for a total of six people. The foils and suspect(s) first washed their hands with unperfumed soap. Five minutes later, they were each handed two tubes to hold in their hands for five minutes. These tubes were then placed in plastic bags or glass jars, one bag/jar per person. Foils and suspects scented their tubes at the same time and for the same duration.

The actual scent identification line-up had to be performed between 15 minutes and two hours after the scenting of the tubes and was prepared by an assistant. Using an assistant ensured that the handler did not know the positions of the suspect's scent—a requirement that was, by this time, standard. Using a pair of tongs, the assistant placed the tubes in different orders in two rows of six so that each row contained the six different scents. The positions of the suspect tubes were random and, again, unknown to the handler.

The handler had the dog smell the corpus delicti and then asked him to retrieve the matching tube in the first row. The handler then asked the dog to retrieve the matching tube from the second row. A match was only declared if the dog chose the suspect's tube in both rows.

An additional rule was also instituted at this time to prevent a dog's memory from playing a role in line-up procedures: a dog was not allowed to perform more than one identification test involving the same suspect within a period of 14 consecutive days. After this 14-day period, the dog could be used in a line-up with the same suspect only if he had performed at least two other, unrelated scent identification line-ups in the intervening time.

THE FITTING-ROOM MURDER

The 1980s saw scent identification line-ups and their results come under fire in Dutch courts. This was particularly clear in one case from the mid-1980s, known as the *Paskamermoord*, or fitting-room murder.*

In 1984, an employee of a boutique in Zaanstad, a town close to Amsterdam, was murdered in the boutique's fitting room. It was a particularly bloody murder. The employee, a young woman, had been gagged with a handkerchief and bound hand and foot with strips of cloth from the fitting-room curtain. Her throat had been cut.

At first, the investigation did not really lead to results—just a lot of loose ends and people contradicting each other. Eventually—nearly two years after the murder—the investigation led to a local bicycle dealer. Two scent identification line-ups were performed with the bicycle dealer as the suspect. In one line-up, the handkerchief that had been used to gag the young woman two years earlier was now used as a corpus delicti. Ten days later, another line-up was performed with the strip of curtain used to tie the girl's ankles. The same dog, Tim, was deployed in both line-ups. Both times, Tim appeared to match the bicycle dealer's scent to the scent of the crime scene evidence. In the first trial, the bicycle dealer was convicted based largely on this scent identification line-up evidence.

He maintained his innocence, saying it was possible he had given the handkerchief to the young woman the evening before the murder. This explanation was not considered credible, as the bike dealer has made an earlier statement that he never had a handkerchief with him. Armed with a new lawyer, the bike dealer appealed.

The new lawyer carefully and critically examined the scent identification procedure and its results. A number of experts were called in, and three major arguments were made against the admissibility of the scent identification evidence. First, the quality of the dog was discussed. Tim, who was used for both line-ups, was also a trained narcotics dog. This was considered to be a disadvantage: it is better to have single-purpose dogs. Second, the quality of the objects used for the line-up was questioned. Both the handkerchief and the strip of curtain were contaminated with blood and possibly corpse scent. On top of this, they had not been preserved properly, and they may have been too old for a reliable scent sample to be collected from them. After all, the line-ups were conducted almost two years after the crime had been committed. Third, the handler knew the position of the tube the bicycle dealer had scented in the line-up; this knowledge could have impacted the results.

The appeal case was dramatic: the scent identification line-up was disqualified, the police investigators were accused of being biased against the bicycle dealer, and a number of loose ends became apparent in the investigation.

Figure 3.4 The dog Tim was used for both scent identification line-ups and narcotics detection. This is now considered to be a disadvantage: it's better to have single-purpose dogs.

The bicycle dealer was acquitted, but the police and also members of the public prosecution remained convinced of his guilt.

Tim's handler, Jan Kaldenbach, wrote about this case. At the time he, too, was convinced of the guilt of the bicycle dealer. In his book, published more than ten years after the case, he was still angry about the way he was treated by the experts and the media.

In 2001, the murder was finally solved. Improved DNA techniques made it possible to match DNA found at the crime scene to a man who, at the time of the murder, had been regarded as a possible suspect. He had been interrogated during the investigation, but the police let him go due to lack of evidence. This man, who had a criminal history, died in 1992. The cold case team accepted the possibility that the handkerchief did belong to the bicycle dealer, who felt the relief of finally being cleared of suspicion.

* Our account of this story comes from Kaldenbach, *K9 Scent Detection*, 127–39.

1990s: 12-Scent and Four-by-Six Line-ups and the Check-First Protocol

The 1990s saw further evolution in the practice and acceptance of K9 scent identification line-ups in the Netherlands. A task group was formed to determine the qualities a dog should have for forensic practice, to discuss the necessity of having the dogs pass an examination before being allowed to perform forensic work (even though a 1949 regulation that required this was still in force), and to critically review the scent identification line-up.

In August 1991, the Dutch government put in place three sets of certification regulations for different kinds of search dogs, one of which was for human-scent search dogs. These regulations described the officially recognized scent identification line-up methods: line-ups of people (which, although no longer used in forensic practice, were still officially permitted); of stainless-steel tubes (which the dog had to retrieve or point out in a specific way); and of scent cloths in glass jars (which the dog had to point out by barking or lying down). The human-scent search dog was expected to perform one of these methods faultlessly in a yearly examination. The dog was then certified to perform scent identification line-ups for forensic purposes using the method for which it was certified.

THE 12-SCENT LINE-UP

The most common method used early in the 1990s was the 12-scent line-up. In this type of line-up, the suspect and 11 foils washed their hands then held a tube or a scent-cloth for five minutes. All line-up participants scented their tube or cloth at the same time, but there were no specific limits on how much time could pass between scenting and performing the line-up. When it came time to do the line-up, an assistant placed the tubes (or the jars containing the scent cloths) in two rows of six. Unlike the two-by-six line-up, only one row contained the suspect's scent in the 12-scent line-up.

The handler let the dog smell the corpus delicti then asked the dog to retrieve or point out the matching scent. The row without the scent of the suspect was a control row: the dog had to smell each of these tubes (or jars) twice without selecting any of them before the handler would recall him. In this way, the dog demonstrated that he was not just choosing any scent. The chance of the dog erroneously pointing to the suspect's scent is further reduced because the total scent comparison was done with 12 scents instead of six. Finally, in this type of line-up, the handler didn't know the position of the suspect's scent, so could not unconsciously influence the dog.

THE FOUR-BY-SIX LINE-UP

Another method used in the 1990s was the four-by-six line-up. In this line-up, the suspect and six foils each held four tubes (or scent cloths) after having washed their hands. In an attempt to increase the reliability of the line-up, it was recommended that foils be of the same gender and ethnicity as the suspect.

The line-up consisted of four rows of six scents each. Two of these rows contained the scent of the suspect and five foils, while the other two contained six foils. The hander asked the dog to compare the scent of the corpus delicti with each of these rows, and to retrieve or point out the matching scents. In a practice situation in which a handler would know that a scent match existed, the dog would be expected to select only the two "suspect" tubes, and to not retrieve or alert to any tubes in the other two rows.

Like in the 12-scent line-up, the handler in the four-by-six line-up was not aware of which rows were the negative controls, nor which tubes or scent cloths were the suspect's. The four-by-six line-up was considered particularly difficult and only a few handlers worked in this way.

THE CHECK-FIRST PROTOCOL

Scent is an elusive study object. The sense of smell is poorly understood, human-scent production is mainly studied (in the context of deodorant production) with the object of eliminating "body odor," and learning behaviors are easier to study in small mammals. For these and other reasons, scent identification line-ups were not scientifically developed or reviewed before 1990.

In the Netherlands in 1991, the biologist G. A. A. Schoon started her investigations on the performance of dogs in identifying humans by scent.[4] In her thesis, she described a number of factors that played a role in the dog's performance such as handler influence, variation in the dog's physical ability over time, and the possible interference of the dog's positive and negative scent associations. Her research motivated the development of a new scent identification protocol, which became an official regulation in the Netherlands in 1997.

In this protocol, seven different scents, of which there are two samples each, are arranged in two rows. Each row contains one sample of each scent. Five of the scents in each row are from foils; one is from the suspect (scent X) and one is from a control person

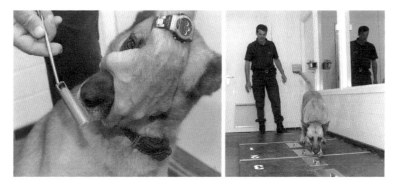

Figure 3.5 A check-first scent identification line-up performed by the dog Spike at the Dutch Police Canine Unit in Nunspeet. Left: Spike is given a lighter, found at the scene of a crime, to smell. Right: Spike searches in the line-up of tubes for a matching scent while his handler observes him closely.

(scent *A*). The position of the scents in both rows is random. The handler does not know which scents belong to the suspect or the control person. Before the dog is allowed to compare the scent of the corpus delicti with the scents in the line-up, the ability of the dog to perform scent identification line-ups is tested by searching for the scent of the control person in both rows. If the dog is able to do this, it also proves that he has no preference or special interest for the scent of the suspect. Only after positively identifying the control person in both rows may the dog compare the scent of the corpus delicti with the remaining six scents in each row. If the dog only responds to the scent of the suspect and ignores all the other scents, this is a positive identification.

2000s: Scent Identification Fraud

"Thousands of Dutch Police Scent Identification Tests Thrown Out." This, or something like it, blared in the headlines of every Dutch newspaper in 2006. "All scent identification line-ups performed by police dogs in the North and East Netherlands District from 1997 to today may no longer be used as evidence in criminal trials," the Board of the Attorney General wrote in a letter to the public prosecutors.[5]

THE MURDERED WIDOW

One of the North and East Netherlands District cases was the 1999 murder of a rich, old widow.* This woman never accepted strangers into her house. Indeed, she only accepted visits from people she did know if they called ahead. After her murder, when no signs of forced entry were found, the group of suspects was immediately limited. The woman clearly knew her killer.

The most obvious suspect was the executor of her recent will. He was president of the foundation that received her money, the bank account of this foundation was in his name, and he had spent her money for private matters, which was contrary to her wishes. He had a key to her house and was a regular guest.

No murder weapon was found in her house. A knife was discovered two days later nearby her house in a doorway, under a porch. It was moved indoors by someone who prevented touching it with his bare hands by covering his hand with his sleeve. Although no blood was found on the knife, it did fit the general type and shape of wound that killed the woman.

Assuming that this knife was the murder weapon, a scent identification line-up was performed using it as the corpus delicti. This identification was performed according to the 1997 regulations: first, two control trials were performed to establish the capacity of the dog to work and to check if the dog had any attractive bias to the suspect's scent. Then two test trials were performed. The dog matched the scent on the knife to the scent of the suspect in both trials. It seemed that the case had been solved with the help of K9 scent identification.

The suspect continued to deny everything. In the lower court he was acquitted due to lack of sufficient evidence. In the appeal court, however, experts testified in detail about scent identification line-ups, as well as some mobile phone evidence that placed the suspect in the area. According to the appeal court, the most convincing piece of evidence was the result of the scent identification line-up using the knife. On the basis of this evidence, the suspect was sentenced to 12 years in December 2000. A win for K9 scent identification, and for justice.

Or was it?

Three years later, advocates for the suspect managed to show that the scent identification line-up performed on the knife had been fraudulent.

The results had been falsified, and in fact DNA tests showed that the knife in question had not been the murder weapon at all. The Dutch Supreme Court decided to reconsider the case in February 2004. While the suspect was ultimately convicted based on new DNA evidence, the fraudulent scent identification line-up tarnished the credibility of K9 scent evidence going forward.

* Our telling of this story is based on the following sources: Dereksen, *Leugens over Louwes* (Lies about Louwes); Haan, *De Deventer moordzaak* (The Deventer murder case); Redactie de Stentor, "Het keukenmes" (The kitchenknife); Rechtspraak, *Deventer moordzaak* (The Deventer Murder Case); Thijssen, "Politie sjoemelde" (Police cheated).

So what happened? In October 2006, in the town of Leeuwarden, two police dog handlers of the North and East Netherlands team of seven dog handlers admitted in court that, for a certain period of time, they hadn't performed scent identification line-ups according to the national regulations. In a number of line-ups performed by this team, the handler knew the position of the suspect's scent. The person who had prepared the line-up, they said, hadn't erased the whiteboard displaying the location of each scent before handler and dog entered the scent identification room. After this admission, the court immediately acquitted the suspects in the case that was then being tried, the seven police dog handlers of North and East Netherlands were placed on leave, and the National Department of Criminal Investigation began investigating the North and East Netherlands K9 unit for perjury and forgery.

At this time in the Netherlands, scent identification regulations required that all line-ups be performed double-blind to avoid influencing the dog. It was found that these regulations had not always been followed by this K9 unit, although their official reports stated that they had.

In November 2007, all seven police dog handlers of the North and East Netherlands team were convicted and sentenced 240 hours of penal labor. Six of the seven handlers were placed on a two-year mandatory leave. Only the dog handler who initially blew the whistle was allowed to continue his duty.

Because of these officers' failure to correctly execute their line-ups and their subsequent falsification of documents, a total of 2,685 police scent identification tests were deemed no longer trustworthy and were invalidated. This led to numerous requests for review of previous convictions. Ultimately, this investigation ruined the reputation of scent identification line-ups in legal contexts in the Netherlands—not because the double-blind, check-first line-ups are unreliable, but because some of the officers who performed them are. One team's incorrect procedure and fraudulent reports destroyed the investigative potential of this invaluable tool in the eyes of the courts. Since 2006, police scent identification line-ups, though still technically admissible as evidence in the Netherlands, are no longer used by Dutch police.

Among professional and amateur dog handlers, however, understanding of the reliability and value of scent identification work remains intact. Today, check-first line-ups are still used in the search dog training program of the *Koninklijke Nederlandse Politie-hond Vereniging*, or Royal Dutch Police Dog Association (KNPV), a non-governmental organization. The KNPV basic search dog certificate program and advanced scent line-up certificates are discussed in detail in the next chapter.

4

KNPV Scent Identification Line-ups

This chapter presents the official scent identification line-up protocol developed and used by Dutch police in the late 1990s: the check-first protocol.[1] This same protocol is used for the KNPV scent identification line-up B certificate today.

As we saw in the last chapter, this protocol is the result of a long history of Dutch police dog work, and ultimately of careful, science-based development. We focus on it here because of its proven value as the only scientifically verified scent identification protocol in the world. It is considered by many to be the gold standard. It is, however, not the only protocol in the world—make sure you are familiar with the line-up protocols in your jurisdiction or club.

Required KNPV Certificates for Scent Identification Dogs

Scent identification certification through the KNPV involves several different levels of training and testing. The line-up B certificate is the most advanced scent identification line-up test in the KNPV training program. To earn it, dogs must first pass their basic search dog and line-up A certifications.

CERTIFICATE FOR BASIC SEARCH DOGS

The KNPV search dogs start with the basic certificate. This is a mandatory program for all search dogs going through KNPV training. Once a dog has its basic certificate, the handler can choose to enter the dog into one of several more specific training disciplines: tracking, area search, rubble search, and scent identification line-up. Each discipline involves two degrees of difficulty, A and B. Unlike the KNPV police dog programs, any breed of dog may be enrolled in the search dog program. You may, for example, train a Jack Russell Terrier or a Great Dane to be a search dog. The only requirements are that the dog be able to complete the exercises proficiently and without compromising his well-being. Because the basic certificate is the foundation for all of the different search disciplines, these exercises will involve certain skills and abilities that may not ultimately be central to your discipline of choice. For instance, dogs destined for scent identification training—which is the least physical of the search dog disciplines—will still need to be able to complete the jumping and climbing exercises with ease.

REQUIRED EXERCISES IN THE BASIC CERTIFICATE FOR SEARCH DOGS

Section 1: Obedience
A. On-leash heeling with tempo changes
B. Off-leash heeling with side changes and noise distraction
C. Off-leash heeling through a group of moving and talking people
D. Staying down during another dog's heeling exercises
E. Off-leash heeling, leaving the dog, and picking him up again
F. Sending the dog out and recalling him
G. Carrying the dog, handing him over to another person, and receiving him again

Section 2: Dexterity on devices

A. Free-jumping over an obstacle

B. Width-jumping

C. Walking on an open staircase

D. Walking across a plank on a catwalk

E. Crawling through a tunnel

F. Walking with handler over unpleasant materials

G. Refusing found food

H. Finding and indicating or retrieving three small objects

Section 3: Search work

A. Finding and indicating a large weapon and housebreaking tool

B. Area searching: searching for and locating a person

C. Tracking: working out a 150 m (492 ft.) track
   with two turns and two articles

D. Scent identification line-up: matching a human-scented
   sample to a matching scented tube, and distinguishing the scented tube from two unscented tubes

KNPV SCENT IDENTIFICATION LINE-UP A CERTIFICATE

After basic search dog certification, dogs in the scent identification stream must pass the scent identification line-up A test. In
this test, dogs are offered the scent of a particular person and then
must find the one matching scent in a line-up of five scent carriers,
each with a different person's scent. The line-up is repeated three
times.

The test uses 20 scent carriers: identical, square, stainless-steel
tubes. Fifteen of these will be used in the line-ups, and five are
extras. One of the extra tubes will be used as the target-scent object
(the training equivalent of a corpus delicti). Five scent donors are
given four tubes each, which they hold in their hands for five
minutes. It is important that all five donors scent their tubes at
the same time. They then then place their scented tubes into a
sterile glass jar. Each donor is assigned their own individual jar.

Figure 4.1 A sorting board as used in the KNPV program being loaded with scented tubes.

This scenting is done between 1 and 24 hours before the sorting test. Note that track layers are not allowed to participate as scent donors in this or other scent-sorting tests as their familiar scents could distract participating dogs.

Before the line-up A test, the judge designates the scent of one of the five scent donors to be the target scent, making the other four donors foils. One of the target-scent tubes and one tube from each of the foils are placed in a row on the sorting platform. About 3 m (10 ft.) away from the end of the sorting platform, the judge gives the handler a jar containing a tube scented with the target scent. The handler offers the tube to the dog to smell, and then sends the dog to the sorting platform to find the matching scent and bring it back to the handler.

The allowed time for each sorting test, including giving the scent, is three minutes. The line-up is repeated three times in different orientations. Before each repetition, the handler gives the dog the scent. To pass the test, the dog must correctly identify the target scent in all three line-ups.

SCENT TUBES

The latest Dutch protocol for collecting human scents involves square, stainless-steel tubes that are 2 cm × 2 cm × 10 cm (0.8 in. × 0.8 in. × 3.9 in.) with wall thicknesses of 0.1 cm to 0.2 cm (0.04 in. to 0.08 in.). The tubes have a neutral scent—that is, before they are given a particular human scent, the only odor they have comes from the material they are made of.

Figure 4.2 A stainless-steel scent tube.

Figure 4.3 A scent identification line-up case with properly stored and labeled materials.

After use, the tubes are placed in a holder and washed in a dishwasher using ordinary detergent at the highest temperature—about 95°C (203°F). They are then boiled in clean water for another hour. They are allowed to dry, then stored in clean, glass jars with twist-off tops. The tubes are scented by asking a person to open the jar, take the tubes out and to hold them in their hands. After a predetermined period of time, this person is asked to return the tubes to the glass jar and to close the lid. The jar is labeled and the tubes are ready for use.

KNPV SCENT IDENTIFICATION LINE-UP B CERTIFICATE

The KNPV scent identification line-up B certificate requires the dog to work out two sorting platforms, each with seven tubes, according to the check-first protocol described in Chapter 3 and in more detail below. Each sorting platform includes a control scent and a target scent. The dog is first given the control scent and must find and retrieve the control-scent tube from each platform. The dog is then given the target scent and must find and retrieve the target-scent tube from each platform. The exercise ends after

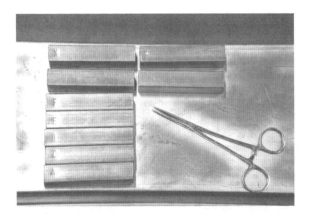

Figure 4.4 Scent tubes prepared for the KNPV scent identification line-up B. The tubes are marked with letters corresponding to the person who scented them: *A* for the control person, *X* for the target person, and *B* through *F* for the foils.

the dog has correctly sorted the tubes four times. Like in the line-up A certificate, the time allowed for each sorting test, including giving the scent, is three minutes.

Setting Up for a Check-First Line-up

Remember that this protocol was initially developed for police work, which means it involved a corpus delicti and a suspect. In a KNPV training and certification context, these are replaced with a scent object and scent carrier that both carry the scent of the same target person. In policing, there is no guarantee that a scent match exists in the line-up—the suspect may not have been involved in the crime, or may not have touched the object used to give the dog scent. This is not the case in a line-up certification test, in which we know there will be a match. To give you an idea of how this protocol can be used in a working context, however, we describe it from a Dutch policing perspective, including the protocol's requirements for recording certain aspects of the line-up in an official report.

PREPARING THE MATERIALS

The preparation of material for a scent identification line-up must be done by an assistant or dog handler certified for the scent identification task. The following materials and participants are needed:

- 1 relevant corpus delicti, properly stored in a closed package and recorded in the scent identification line-up's official report
- 14 identical scent carriers (usually stainless-steel tubes)
- 1 control object (ideally made of material similar to the corpus delicti)
- 7 sterile containers to store scent carriers after handling
- 1 sterile container to store the control object after handling
- 7 participants:
  › 1 target-scent person
  › 1 control-scent person
  › 5 foils

Figure 4.5 Hands holding tubes in preparation for a scent identification line-up.

The seven participants each hold two scent carriers for 5 to 10 minutes. It is not necessary for participants to wash hands prior to handling the scent carriers, since the line-up procedure includes a check on the attractiveness of any scent or odor for the dog. It is also unnecessary that scent carriers be scented by being held in participants hands. It is, however, necessary that all carriers are scented in the same way and at the same time. If, for example, a suspect were to refuse to hold the carriers in their hands, the scent carriers may be scented using another method, which must then also be performed by the control person and foils. Whatever the method, it needs to be recorded in the official report.

THE SCENT IDENTIFICATION PLATFORM

Scent identification platforms used in the Netherlands in policing contexts (Figure 3.1) are made of wood and coated with material that prevents the dog from slipping. Each platform is 1 m (3.3 ft.) wide and 5.5 m (18 ft.) long, and includes seven numbered, stainless-steel plates, each 50 cm (20 in.) apart. The plates' dimensions are 15 cm × 35 cm (6 in. × 12 in.), each with an affixed clamping mechanism to hold the tubes.

Each clamping mechanism is activated by a numbered switch that matches each plate. When a dog indicates a particular scent tube by performing its

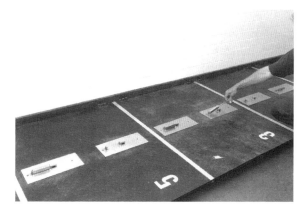

Figure 4.6 A scent identification platform as used by the Dutch police.

alert behavior, the handler, who is standing near the switchbox, can release the tube from the clamping mechanism, allowing the dog to retrieve it.

The wooden platforms and metal plates are cleaned regularly. Between trials, the plates are sprayed with clean water and wiped clean. The plates can also be removed for thorough cleaning in a dishwasher.

After the carriers have been scented, they are collected. The control object is collected separately. The carriers and the control object are coded on the packaging: *A* for the control person's scent carriers and control object, *B* through *F* for the foils' scent carriers, and *X* for the target person's scent carriers. The line-up assistant notes the names that go with each code for the registration system only (these names will not be mentioned in the official report for privacy reasons). The genders and ethnicities of the people involved are also noted for registration purposes. The control person is described in the line-up's official report, and their name is registered in the scent identification line-up registration system.

PREPARING THE LINE-UP

The scents are presented according to one of 36 different sequence schemes (Table 4.1), each of which has been assigned a two-digit

Figure 4.7 A scent identification line-up storage room, containing all the materials necessary for training.

Table 4.1 Scent sequence schemes for platforms 1 and 2

2-DIGIT CODE	SCENT SEQUENCE IN ROWS 1 AND 2	2-DIGIT CODE	SCENT SEQUENCE IN ROWS 1 AND 2	2-DIGIT CODE	SCENT SEQUENCE IN ROWS 1 AND 2
11	1. A X B E C F D 2. C D X F A B E	31	1. B A D X C F E 2. D E B F C X A	51	1. X F D C B E A 2. C A X F D B E
12	1. D E X A B F C 2. B A F D C E X	32	1. C E B X A F D 2. C A B E X D F	52	1. X A B C E F D 2. F E A X B D C
13	1. E B X C F A D 2. C E B A F D X	33	1. E D C F X A B 2. F B A X E D C	53	1. C B A D X F E 2. X F E C A D B
14	1. E X A B F C D 2. B E A F X C D	34	1. X A B F C D E 2. F C D E A X B	54	1. A B C D E F X 2. D C X B A F E
15	1. F E D B C X A 2. B C A E X F D	35	1. B X A D C E F 2. A X F E D C B	55	1. E A C B D F X 2. D E F X B A C
16	1. X C B A F D E 2. A D X F C E B	36	1. D C F B E X A 2. A D F X B C E	56	1. C D E X F B A 2. E C F A D X B
21	1. E D B X C A F 2. D C A F B E X	41	1. C F X E B A D 2. A X B C F E D	61	1. F A C X B D E 2. X A B F D E C
22	1. B C X D A F E 2. E B C D F A X	42	1. D E B F A C X 2. X A B C F D E	62	1. B X F C E D A 2. E F B A C D X
23	1. E B C F X A D 2. A B F C X D E	43	1. F E D A B C X 2. B E X D C A F	63	1. A C B F X D E 2. D X E B C F A
24	1. B C X A F E D 2. A E B C X F D	44	1. D X B F A C E 2. B C D A E X F	64	1. A D F E B X C 2. X B C A E F D
25	1. D F A B E X C 2. X D F C E B A	45	1. X E F B A C D 2. B A D X F E C	65	1. C E A D X B F 2. E X B C D A F
26	1. F B C X E A D 2. B F E D C X A	46	1. F E X A B C D 2. C D E F A B X	66	1. A C E B D X F 2. D X B F E C A

code in which each digit is between 1 and 6. These scent sequences and their numbered codes are standardized in the Netherlands. The assistant determines the sequence to be used by throwing a six-sided die twice. Using clean tongs, the assistant then installs the scent carriers in the two platforms according to the sequence determined by their dice throw.

It is imperative that the dog handler and dog be absent during the preparation of the line-up. To avoid influencing the dog's choice, the handler must not know the position of the different scents, and must certify that this is the case in the scent identification line-up's official report.

THE SCENT IDENTIFICATION ROOM

Scent identification rooms for police line-ups should be purpose built and reserved for scent identification. The entire room should be regularly cleaned with ordinary detergents and aired out.

In the Netherlands, scent identification rooms contain two platforms, approximately 3 m (10 ft.) apart. Each platform has its own switchbox to operate the tube clamps. Each room also has a whiteboard to register the location of each of the different scents on each platform, a table or shelf to hold the glass jars with the tubes, and a red/green signaling system connected to an

Figure 4.8 A scent identification room at the training institute for specialist dogs of the Dutch police in Nunspeet.

observation room, which looks onto the scent identification room through one-way glass. The whiteboard must be cleaned before the handler and dog enter the room. The signal is operated by someone in the observation room who knows the position of each scent. This system is used to tell the handler, who is working double-blind, whether the dog has indicated the expected tube (i.e., the tube scented by the suspect or target person) or not.

KEEPING A RECORD OF LINE-UP RESULT

In the Dutch policing protocol for scent identification, the results of a scent identification line-up would be recorded in two main ways: in an official report, written under oath of office; and in the scent identification registration system. It is also advisable to keep a video record of scent identification line-ups.

The official report contains a description of the line-up material and how it was prepared; descriptions of the control person, the control object, and how long it was scented; a record of whether the suspect participated freely in the scent collection by holding the scent carriers or if the scents were collected in a different way; information on the assistant and his procedure; a record of the scent sequence scheme used; a description of how each step in the procedure was performed; and the result of each step. The handler includes in the report a declaration under oath that her dog is unfamiliar with the control person and that she was unaware of the position of any of the scents in the line-up. She also provides a sworn statement as to whether her dog exhibited any scent preferences in steps 1 and 2. The official report is co-signed by the assistant(s) involved.

The result of every line-up is entered into the scent identification registration system either by filling in a form or using a software package developed for keeping this type of record. The commander of the K9 unit should regularly review this registry to perform continuous quality control on the dogs that perform scent identification line-ups. Even if you are not working in a policing context, keeping a record of your dog's performance on scent identification line-ups can be a helpful training tool. Setting up a simple but effective system for data collection will help you track your dog's progress throughout his training and scent identification career. The KNPV does not describe any best practices for data collection in the training or performance of scent identification, so we include none here. You may, however, find our data collection strategies for detection work (Chapter 10) helpful and adaptable to scent identification work.

Performing the Line-up

All line-ups follow the same five-step flow chart, described below and in Table 4.2. Before we get into the step-by-step specifics of performing a scent identification line-up, it's important to understand a few preliminary points.

Every line-up should be performed in a place that is familiar to the dog, preferably in a room that is designated for performing scent identification line-ups. The room should have a fairly stable temperature at all times and should be a place where the dog is commonly trained. When performing the line-up, ensure that only the people necessary to executing the line-up are present while the dog is working. Those who are present should position themselves in such a way that neither the dog nor the handler can see them, such as behind a pane of one-way glass.

A single scent identification line-up may only contain the scent of a single suspect. If there is more than one suspect, a separate line-up must be prepared for each of them. If the same dog is used in successive line-ups for multiple suspects, it is necessary to use new foils and controls for each line-up.

In some policing contexts, you may be working with several corpus delicti and a single suspect. Only one corpus delicti may be used in a single line-up. However, if no scent similarity was found in the first line-up, you may perform subsequent line-ups with other corpora delicti and the same dog. It is important in these subsequent line-ups that all the scents in the line-up are the same as in the earlier line-up, but on fresh carriers. Performing subsequent line-ups is not allowed if the first line-up results in a scent similarity, a disqualification, or an incorrect procedure.

It is also possible to use a single corpus delicti for several line-ups—for instance, if there is more than one suspect to assess. In these cases, the corpus delicti can be used in subsequent line-ups with the same dog or with a different dog. All line-ups involving a single corpus delicti have to be performed within 8 hours of it being unsealed. Dogs used in line-ups involving a "used" corpus delicti—that is, one that has not been freshly unsealed—must be trained with this in mind.

When performing a line-up, a dog should work systematically. This means, especially in the first steps of a line-up, that the dog should begin a position 1 on the scent identification platform and proceed down the platform to position 7, smelling each scent along the way.

The dog handler may terminate a line-up at any point, resulting in a dog's disqualification from working on that particular line-up. The dog will also be disqualified from the line-up if it fails to match the control scent, if it does not smell all of the carriers in the line-up, or if it shows a special interest in the suspect scent.

Finally, if a dog either finds a scent similarity between the corpus delicti and a suspect or has been disqualified because it showed special interest in the scent of the suspect, that dog may not be used in any scent identification line-ups involving that suspect's scent for 14 days. During these 14 days, the dog should have at least two successful line-up training sessions.

STEP 1: CONTROL SCENT, PLATFORM 1

Once a line-up has been set up, the handler and dog enter the room and prepare to perform the scent identification. The assistant positions himself such that the dog cannot see him when the search is in progress. The handler approaches platform 1 with her dog. She lets the dog smell the control object, then lets it search the platform freely to find the matching scent. The handler may give the dog the control object scent once more in this first platform search if necessary; this is the only step in which a scent may be presented twice.

When the dog performs its alert behavior (which will be described on the dog's training certificate), the handler signals the assistant. If the dog has indicated the control scent, the assistant gives a green signal. The handler may then give the dog its standard reward for a correct response (also described on the dog's training certificate). The team may then move on to step 2.

If the dog fails to indicate the control scent, the assistant gives a red signal. This means that the dog is disqualified from the line-up. This disqualification is recorded in the official report. The dog will also be disqualified at this step if it smells all of the scent carriers in the line-up but does not indicate any scent, or if it does not smell all of the carriers in the line-up.

STEP 2: CONTROL SCENT, PLATFORM 2

The procedure from step 1 is repeated on platform 2. If the dog correctly identifies the control, dog and handler move on to step 3. An incorrect response, lack of response, or incomplete search on this platform will lead to disqualification. The dog may only smell the control object once in step 2.

STEP 3: ASSESSMENT OF SCENT PREFERENCE

After the dog has responded to the control scent in both rows, the handler evaluates the dog's behavior in steps 1 and 2. If the handler concludes that the dog has shown special interest for one of the scents on a platform, he must let the assistant know. If this scent belongs to the suspect, the dog is disqualified from the line-up. If the scent does not belong to the suspect, the line-up may continue.

The handler records the dog's performance and behavior on the control trials in the official report and indicates whether or not the line-up will continue with this dog. If the line-up is to continue, the assistant ensures that the control scents are removed from both platforms. In some cases—for instance, when a dog's reward is to retrieve the tube it indicates—the control scents will already have been removed.

STEP 4: SUSPECT SCENT, PLATFORM 1

Both platforms now consist of six scents total. The handler returns with his dog to platform 1. He lets the dog smell the corpus delicti, then search the platform freely for a matching scent. The handler may only present the corpus delicti to the dog once.

If the dog responds to one of the scents, the handler gives a signal. If this is the scent of the suspect, the assistant gives a green signal, the dog is rewarded in the usual manner, and the team moves on to step 5.

If the dog responds to the scent of one of the foils, the assistant gives a red signal and the line-up is terminated. In this case, the result is recorded in the official report and in the registration system as "incorrect procedure." If, however, the dog has worked systematically, smelled all of the scent carriers, and indicated none, the result is recorded as "no scent similarity." If the dog has not smelled all of the carriers and does not indicated any particular scent, the result is still recorded as "no scent similarity," unless the dog has systematically not smelled the scent of the suspect. If this is the case, it must be specially noted in the official report.

STEP 5: SUSPECT SCENT, PLATFORM 2

If the dog made a scent match on platform 1, the procedure from step 4 is repeated on platform 2. The handler lets the dog smell the corpus delicti once, then lets it search platform 2 for a matching scent. If the dog again responds to the scent of the suspect, the result of the

Table 4.2 Scent identification line-up procedure summary

STEP	PLATFORM	SCENT OBJECT	DOG'S SCENT SELECTION	RESULT
1	1	Control object (matches scent A)	A	Continue to step 2
			B, C, D, E, F, or X	Disqualification
			No response	Disqualification
2	2	Control object (matches scent A)	A	Continue to step 3
			B, C, D, E, F, or X	Disqualification
			No response	Disqualification
3	1 & 2	–	–	Handler assessment: No special interest in scent X
				Continue to step 4
			–	Handler assessment: Special interest in scent X
				Disqualification
4	1	Corpus delicti (matches scent X)	X	Continue to step 5
			B, C, D, E, or F	Incorrect procedure
			No response	No scent similarity
5	2	Corpus delicti (matches scent X)	X	Scent similarity between object and suspect
			B, C, D, E, or F	Incorrect procedure
			No response	No scent similarity

Note: A = control scent. *X* = suspect scent.

entire five-step line-up is recorded as "scent similarity between object and suspect." If the dog responds to a foil in this row, the final result is "incorrect procedure." If the dog does not respond to any of the scents in this row, the final result is "no scent similarity."

Now you know how to carry out a check-first scent identification line-up—but how do you train for it? We'll address this in Chapter 5.

5

Training Dogs in Scent Identification Line-ups

This chapter describes the training program that has been used by the canine unit of the KLPD to train dogs to perform the scent identification line-up according to the KNPV standards.[1] This training program continues to be a common way to train dogs for KNPV certification. It consists of seven steps that build in difficulty as the dog becomes more and more adept at solving scent problems. These seven steps are schematically represented in Figure 4.0. The chapter also gives an overview of two variations on this standard training, which are becoming increasingly popular.

The reward system used in this training program is called the "tube method." In the tube method, human scents are collected on stainless-steel tubes, and these tubes are clamped onto a scent identification platform. If a dog makes a correct scent match, the line-up assistant rewards him by releasing the tube for him to retrieve. An incorrect indication is never rewarded by releasing a tube. Other reward methods may be used instead, but these methods may lead to specific problems that are not discussed here.

Like the KNPV line-ups described in Chapter 4, this training does not involve a corpus delicti or suspect scent, but rather a

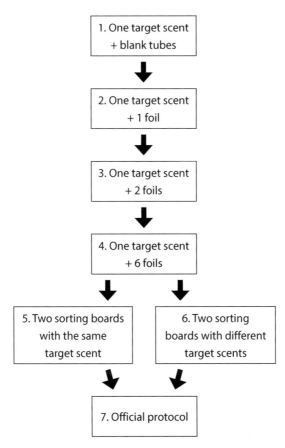

Figure 5.1 The seven steps of basic scent identification line-up training.

target person who has scented both a scent object and target-scent carriers. While the handler should not know where the target scent is in the line-up, he will know that the target scent is present in the line-up and that the dog should be able to find a match. In a real, working situation, this would not be the case.

Building Up Complexity

Training usually begins with a single platform of scents. Over the course of the first four training steps, the combination of scents used becomes increasingly complex. In step 1, one target-scent carrier is presented alongside six unscented tubes. In step 2, the unscented tubes are replaced with tubes scented by the same individual foil. In step 3, two foils are used to scent the foil tubes. In step 4, all seven tubes carry unique scents. Over the course of these four training steps, the handler also trains the dog using different types of target-scent objects (the equivalent of a corpus delicti in a policing context). The dog is ready to move on to step five only after he can reliably pick out the appropriate scent carrier from a full seven-scent platform and take the initial scent from a reasonable variety of target-scent objects.

Training the dog for the official, check-first scent identification line-up protocol begins in step 5, when the dog starts working with two scent platforms. In step 5, the dog must make a scent match on the first platform and repeat the match on the second platform. In step 6, two target scents are used: one for platform 1 and another for platform 2. The dog must make the correct match on both platforms according to the target scent used. Steps 5 and 6 may be trained in succession or simultaneously.

Finally, in step 7, the dog is trained in official protocol. He must first match the scent of a control object to the appropriate scent carrier on both platforms, then do the same with a target scent.

Training looks neat and tidy when you separate it into seven simple steps, but it isn't always so tidy in reality. While these steps work well as general guidelines for training, handlers should be prepared to find that their dog does not always progress linearly from one stage to the next. In fact, such linear progression is unadvisable. It is recommended that handlers regularly go back and retrain earlier steps over the course of a dog's complete scent identification line-up training.

Seven-Step Training for Scent Identification Line-ups

Below, we include a basic method for each of the seven training steps, including specific training objectives and the training timeframe in which they should be achieved. This timeframe is based on an assumption of approximately three training sessions a day, five days a week. As a general rule, when moving from a simpler to a more advanced step, handlers are advised to first let the dog make a scent match at the simpler level, and then repeat the same choice (using the same scents) at the higher level of difficulty. The higher level becomes the training baseline only when the dog consistently performs the scent match correctly at this level.

STEP 1: THE DOG LEARNS TO SEARCH FOR A SCENTED TUBE

Objective: The dog is consistently able to take the scent from a target object and correctly indicate the target-scent carrier from among six other scent carriers, all of which are unscented. When searching for the target tube, the dog should ignore the unscented tubes. The dog should be persistent in his choice of scent carrier, making the same choice at least five consecutive times.

Timeframe: Maximum of 2 weeks.

Method: This step involves simply getting the dog used to the task at hand—that is, searching for and matching a target-scent carrier with the scent of a target object. At this point, the dog has not yet learned to work with the scent identification platform and its exposed tubes and clamping mechanisms, so the trainer or an assistant places seven

Figure 5.2 Large, unscented objects on the line-up platform. A scented tube is hidden behind one of them for the dog to find.

heavy objects on a platform (Figure 5.2), then hides the target tube in one of these objects. Eventually, unscented tubes are hidden in the other objects. The scent carriers should be well hidden so the dog is encouraged to use his nose in his search. Before each trial, the dog is given the target object to smell.

At first, the dog should be allowed to watch the scent carrier being hidden. After the dog is able to reliably retrieve the scent carrier, the trainer or assistant should begin to hide the carrier while the dog is not watching, or should mislead the dog by pretending to hide the carrier in one place, but actually hide it in another. Initially, the target-scent carrier should be "warm"—that is, very recently scented—and placed on the platform by the person who scented it. As training at this stage continues, the trainer should use progressively "colder" scent carriers (up to 2 days old).

It is best to add the six unscented carriers to the platform after the dog has already been allowed to search for and find the scented carrier on his own. This way, the dog will know which scent he is after. When present, the unscented tubes should be fixed so that the dog cannot retrieve an incorrect tube. After some time, the scented tube should also be fixed to teach the dog to persist in his choice.

Once the dog reliably makes the correct choice of scent carrier, the objects used to hide the carriers are removed from the platform, ex-posing the tubes. All tubes are now fixed, and the dog must walk along the platform and indicate a choice. The dog can be encouraged with verbal praise and/or vigorous petting when he responds to the correct scent carrier.

In all cases, the dog must make his choice independently and without the help of the trainer. The trainer must be careful not to react to the dog's behavior until he has made a choice, allowing a moment to pass between the dog's initial response and the trainer's reaction or praise.

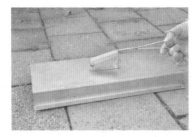 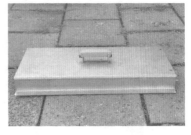

Figure 5.3 Left: A scent tube is placed on a simple, non-clamping sorting board as used in KNPV programs. Right: The tube is fixed to the sorting board with a metal pin to prevent the dog from removing it from the board.

Including this short pause encourages the dog to persist in his choice, which will be necessary for future work in which the handler will not know the positions of the specific scent carriers.

STEP 2: THE DOG LEARNS TO DISTINGUISH A TARGET SCENT FROM ONE OTHER SCENT

Objective: The dog is consistently able to take the scent from a target object and correctly indicate the matching scent carrier from among six other scent carriers, which have all been scented by a single foil. The dog should be persistent in his choice of scent carrier, making the same choice at least five consecutive times.

Timeframe: Maximum of 2 weeks.

Method: There are two main training methods that may be used in step 2.

1. **The "older foil" method:** You may begin training step 2 using foil scent carriers that are much older or "colder" than the target scent carrier. The foil carriers may have been scented several days, weeks, or even months earlier than those of the target person. Gradually, you can begin to use progressively warmer foil carriers. Eventually, the foil and target carriers should be scented at the same time.

2. **The "weaker foils" method:** In this method, the foil carriers are scented at the same time as the target carrier, but for a much shorter time. For example, if the target person holds their carrier for five minutes, the foil only holds theirs for a few seconds. Gradually, you can increase the time for which the foil scents their carriers until foil and target carriers are scented for an equal amount of time.

A disadvantage of both methods, and of step 2 as a whole, is that the dog may learn to simply look for the odd tube out: the freshest or the strongest, or the one that doesn't smell like all the others. It is therefore necessary to pass through step 2 quickly to prevent the dog from fixing on a poor search strategy. If this does become the dog's primary strategy, it can cause issues later in training, and the dog will have to be retrained to use a different strategy.

STEP 3: THE DOG LEARNS TO DISTINGUISH A TARGET SCENT FROM TWO OTHER SCENTS

Objective: The dog is consistently able to take the scent from a target object and correctly indicate the matching scent carrier from among six other scent carriers, some of which have been scented by one foil and some by another. The dog should be persistent in his choice of scent carrier, making the same choice at least five consecutive times.

Figure 5.4 In this KNPV line-up, the dog correctly chooses the target scent (in the middle), distinguishing it from the scented tubes on either side.

Timeframe: Maximum of 2 weeks.

Method: Once the dog can make a correct choice among tubes scented by a single foil, the scent of a second foil can be introduced. If this creates a problem for the dog, you may begin training step 3 with either the "older foils" or "weaker foils" methods from step 2, this time using two foils instead of one. You need not use significantly older or weaker foil carriers—a day or two older or a few seconds weaker should be enough.

Begin by introducing only one scent carrier with the second foil's scent into the line-up. In this initial line-up setting, there should be one target tube, five tubes from the first foil, and one tube from the second foil. Once the dog can consistently make the correct choice in this setting, further second-foil carriers can be introduced until there are three carriers from each foil.

STEP 4: THE DOG LEARNS TO DISTINGUISH A TARGET SCENT FROM SIX OTHER SCENTS

Objective: The dog is able to take the scent from a target object and correctly indicate the matching scent carrier from among six other scent carriers, each of which has been scented by a different foil. The dog should be persistent in his choice of scent carrier. The dog must make a correct first choice 80% of the time and maintain this level of performance for two weeks.

Timeframe: Approximately 3 months.

Method: Stepping up from 2 to 6 foil scents should be relatively simple for the dog, but the "older foil" and "weaker foil" methods can be used, as they were in step 3, if the dog requires them. Using strategic repetition will also help the dog. For example, the target-scent carrier can initially be placed in position 2 or 3, allowing the dog to come across only one or two other scents before reaching the target scent. Before asking the dog to repeat his choice, the target scent can be moved to somewhere near the end of the row, forcing the dog to smell many different scents before reaching the correct tube. Because the dog already knows the scent he is looking for from the first trial, he will be better able to ignore the foil scents in the second.

After the dog is able to consistently make the correct choice using this strategic repetition method, you should begin to position the scents randomly. (Consider throwing dice to truly randomize the order of scents! See Table 4.1 in Chapter 4.) This will prevent the dog from building up expectations that will ultimately not help him in his work.

Success in step 4, as in the other steps, is based on a high performance average, with the dog making the correct choice at least 80% of the time, counting only first choices. Hitting this average may become more difficult as the difficulty of each step increases. The dog must learn to handle mistakes in step 4. He must not panic when he is given a verbal reprimand, but continue searching. The trainer or handler must also learn to handle mistakes and accept nonrecognitions. She must try to analyze where mistakes come from, and respond in ways

Figure 5.5 A complete row of seven scented tubes.

Figure 5.6 A complete, seven-scent line-up. Use the schemas in Chapter 4 to determine the order of your scent carriers. It is important to place the tubes on the sorting board in the correct order.

that will help the dog succeed. If the dog reacts strongly to one of the foil scents, for example, remove this scent from the row.

Handlers should be careful not to force a dog to make a recognition that he hasn't made on his own or be quick to punish a dog that has made a mistake. Using force will teach the dog to start paying attention to the handler rather than the scents. He will be looking for cues to prevent the handler from punishing him, and this will cause him to stop using his nose.

STEP 5: THE DOG LEARNS TO INDICATE THE TARGET SCENT ON TWO PLATFORMS

Objective: The dog is consistently able to take the scent from a sample scent object and correctly indicate the matching scent carrier on a platform of seven individual scents. The dog must then repeat his correct choice on a second platform of identical scents arranged in a different order. The dog should be persistent in his choice of scent carrier on both platforms, being correct at least 80% of the time.

Timeframe: Alternating with step 6, approximately 4 months.

Figure 5.7 Top left: A dog smells the target-scented tube on one of the line-up platforms. Top right: To convince himself, he smells the tube again… Bottom left: …and then takes the tube from the platform and brings it to his handler. Bottom right: The dog brings the tube to his handler and waits expectantly for his reward.

Method: Step 5 is a simple continuation of step 4, adding a second platform. The dog must learn to go from one platform to the other, take the scent of the target object before searching each platform, and begin in position 1 both times.

STEP 6: THE DOG LEARNS TO CHANGE TARGET SCENTS BETWEEN PLATFORMS

Aim: The dog is consistently able to take the scent from a target object and correctly indicate the matching scent carrier on a platform of seven individual scents. The dog must then take the scent from a second target object (scented by a different target person) and correctly indicate its matching scent carrier on a second platform of seven scents. The dog should be persistent in his choice of scent carrier on both platforms, being correct at least 80% of the time.

Timeframe: Alternating with step 5, approximately 4 months.

Method: The training method is the same as step 5 except that, before the second platform, the dog is presented with a second target object that carries a different scent from the first. This second target person should be assigned from among the foils, and their scent should be present on both platforms. In the beginning, this second object can be a scented tube or another object familiar to the dog. As training progresses, the dog should be presented with a variety of scent objects for both choices, some familiar and some not.

If a dog cannot make a choice with your first scent, don't force a recognition. Switch to the next scent. If necessary, use a target object that the dog finds easier to work with or present the unfamiliar target object alongside a scented tube with a matching scent. Always make sure you have more than enough material when starting a training session, and be prepared to accept that things may not always work out.

If the dog isn't able to make his first choice easily, fall back to step 4 and allow him to make the problem scent match a number of times at this lower difficulty. Keep in mind that, after repeating a scent match several times with the same scent, a dog will at first find it difficult to switch to a new scent. Return to step 6 only when the dog no longer struggles to make his first choice using the problem scent.

If changing scents continues to be difficult for the dog, you may try using a very short row of only three or four different scents on platform 2. If this goes well, try asking the dog to repeat his platform 2 choice on platform 1. You may take the dog out of the room between the first and second choices to let him get a fresh nose, or you may hide the second object somewhere in the training room and let the dog find it using his nose.

As the dog becomes comfortable in step 6, the exercise can be expanded to involve three or four different target objects, each scented by a different person whose scent is also included on the platforms.

STEP 7: THE DOG LEARNS TO FOLLOW THE OFFICIAL PROTOCOL

Objective: The dog is able to work on two platforms, each containing the same seven scents. The dog can consistently take the scent from a control object and correctly indicate the matching scent carrier on both platforms. The dog can then take the scent from a target object and correctly indicate its matching scent carrier on the same two platforms. The dog will be able to work with different types and ages of scent objects, and will be able to work with objects that have their own odor in addition to the human scent. The dog must make a correct first choice 80% of the time using freshly scented objects and maintain this level of performance for a month.

Timeframe: The remainder of the dog's working life.

Method: Step 7 is a continuation of step 6. The dog is given the target object only if he first correctly indicates the control scent on both platforms. As in step 6, begin with control objects and target objects that the dog finds easy to work with, then progress to more difficult objects. If certain objects, additional scents or odors, or weak scents create problems for the dog, you may begin by having someone familiar to the dog scent these objects. You may then begin using the scents of people unknown to the dog, but be sure at first to present these scents on objects with which the dog is familiar.

Once the dog is 80% reliable using freshly scented objects, he is ready for KNPV certification.

Variations on Standard Line-up Training

There are two main variations on the standard training method: the short-long method, and the familiar-unfamiliar method. Both of these variations allow the dog to skip steps 2 and 3 of the basic training method, which risk encouraging the dog to use an "odd-tube-out" search strategy rather than learning to actually identify particular scents. These variations can also be used to help dogs learn the official line-up search strategies and techniques before applying them to complex scent problems, thus not overloading them with new information as training progresses. Both of these variant methods have been used successfully to train young dogs.

THE SHORT-LONG METHOD

The short-long method has become increasingly popular, in part because, as noted, it makes it possible to skip steps 2 and 3 in the standard method. You can also use the short row to focus and improve on different training objectives such as being persistent with a choice, searching for a long time, always beginning a search with the first scent on a platform, working with unfamiliar scent objects, handling mistakes, working with a leash, and allowing the handler to move alongside the dog. Training these points will measurably improve the dog's work in the second row and in complete scent line-ups.

SHORT-LONG LINE-UP TRAINING

In this method, one platform is prepared as in step 1 of standard training: one scented tube among six unscented tubes. This is the "short" row, having only one scent to which the dog can react. The second platform is prepared as in step 4, with one target tube and six different and equally scented foil tubes. This is the "long" row. The target scent is the same in both rows. It is important, in this method, that all of the carriers in the long row be equally scented, and that none are older or weaker than the others.

When the dog responds well to the scented tube in the first row, you can immediately continue with the second row. This is, in many ways, a simple repetition, but the dog is now confronted with a number of other scents that he has to ignore. If this causes difficulty, you may begin with a long row that contains fewer than seven individual scents.

Once the dog is able to consistently make the right choice in this arrangement, you can replace the unscented tubes on the first platform with scented tubes. This is equivalent to the setup of step 5 in standard training. If necessary, the number of scents in the row can be incrementally increased. You may also reuse a target scent that was used in a prior (successful) training trial involving a short row. This should be done during the same training session, in trials perhaps half an hour apart. When the suspect scent is presented for the second time, the dog should be asked to find the matching scent carrier in a complete row containing seven different scents.

THE FAMILIAR-UNFAMILIAR METHOD

The familiar-unfamiliar method is an adaptation of a method described in the book *Honden leren sorteren en speuren* (Teaching dogs to sort and track).[2] The idea behind this method is to use the scent of the handler himself, followed by the scents of familiar people, and finally by the scents of unfamiliar people in all advanced training stages, allowing the dog to learn and apply increasingly complicated concepts at different levels of difficulty.

The first stages of training using this method, however, use only the handler's scent. The dog is very familiar with the scent of his handler, and will easily recognize this scent amidst other scents. By using this scent, the dog can easily be taught basic scent identification skills, and will quickly progress to step 4 of standard training without fixating on incorrect cues or strategies. As with the short-long method, steps 2 and 3 can be skipped.

Once the dog's search strategies and techniques have been solidified, the training continues with variations on the later stages of standard training, each using the handler's scent, familiar scents, and unfamiliar scents.

FAMILIAR TOY TRAINING

The first step in this method differs from the standard method. In this method, the handler's scent is used to first teach the dog the proper method of searching a line-up. This step also involves using a toy that is familiar to the dog, and with which he enjoys playing. This toy should be something the dog can shake like prey, such as a tennis ball in a long sock. The dog's interest in the toy should be established long before training begins. The best way we have found to stimulate a dog's interest in such a toy is by throwing it low over the ground, and later into high grass or among trees so the dog can search for it. After searching and finding the toy, the dog may play with it as he pleases. When the dog loses interest in the toy, the handler recalls him and exchanges the toy for a treat. Once the dog's interest in the toy is well established, the handler keeps the toy and only uses it during training sessions.

Rather than using a line-up platform, the first training sessions in this method can be conducted using a number of boxes or baskets placed upside-down in a row. Keep the training toy and a scent object in your pocket for an hour, then place the toy under the first box.

In a real line-up, a dog will need to smell a corpus delicti or target-scent object before searching for a matching scent. However, smelling a scent object when asked is not an automatic behavior for a dog, and must be trained. To do this, hold the dog's snout with one hand, and hold the scent object in front of the dog's nose with the other for at least half a minute. This should be coupled with the command "smell." To motivate the dog to smell, you may make sniffing noises. Then reward the dog by taking him to the first box and allowing him to find and play with his toy.

Continue training by hiding the toy under subsequent boxes in the row. Have the dog smell the scent object, then search each box in order until he finds his toy. If the dog is doing well, other articles containing the handler's scent can be hidden under the boxes. Eventually, the toy and other articles can be replaced with steel scent tubes.

In the initial training sessions, the dog is also gradually but explicitly taught the crucial line-up skills of beginning with the first scent in the line-up, working in a straight line, and smelling every scent carrier.

FAMILIAR-UNFAMILIAR LINE-UP TRAINING

After toy training, we can begin with the real line-up training. In the familiar-unfamiliar method, line-up training exercises are repeated at three levels:

1. Searching for the handler's scent
2. Searching for a familiar, friendly person's scent

3. Searching for the scent of an unfamiliar person

At each level, there are five exercises, (a) to (e), with increasing levels of difficulty. As in the standard training method, each exercise involves the dog finding the target scent among a number of other tubes that are:

a. Unscented

b. Scented with the same weak scent

c. Scented with the same strong scent

d. Scented with different weak scents

e. Scented with different strong scents.

Exercises (b) and (c) involve a single foil while exercises (d) and (e) involve multiple foils. In exercises (b) and (d), the foils' scents are weaker than the target scent. In exercises (c) and (e), they are the same strength as the target scent. The dog must successfully complete each exercise ([a] through [e]) at every level (1 through 3), only progressing from one level to the next after he can consistently complete all exercises at the lower level.

After the dog is competent at all exercises at the highest level, he can progress straight to steps 6 and 7 of the basic training protocol.

Regardless of the training method they choose, handlers should expect training to advance nonlinearly and be ready to go back to earlier steps when the dog requires it. More than this, however, many handlers will encounter certain common issues in training that are not addressed in these seven steps and require special attention. These topics are addressed in Chapter 6.

6

Troubleshooting Common Problems in Scent Identification

Few things in life are certain, but one thing is for sure: you will encounter roadblocks when training your dog in scent identification line-ups. When problems do arise, whatever they are, remember two things. First, it is advantageous to work in a group and to discuss problems prior to doing something about them. Others often see things a handler himself has not yet noticed. Discussing and thoroughly analyzing a problem with experienced colleagues often leads to a direct solution. Second, some problems are best addressed outside the usual scent identification room or arena in order to prevent the dog from developing (temporary) negative associations.

In this chapter, we look at some of the most common problems you may encounter when training your dog in scent identification line-ups.

Form and Content Problems

The common problems in scent identification training can be roughly categorized as form problems and content problems. Form problems involve the technique with which the line-up is performed: taking scent well, performing the line-up correctly and systematically, making persistent indications, and so on. Content problems involve a dog having trouble working with the scents in the line-up, perhaps because the scent carriers are too cold, because the target object is unfamiliar to the dog, or because scents have been contaminated by other scents or odors that make them difficult to work with. In other words, form problems have to do with technique or training while content problems have to do with the difficulty of the scent problem or the dog's ability to make a match.

The same issue—for example, failing to pick up a scent well—may be the result of a form problem, a content problem, or both. This can make it difficult to pinpoint exactly what your dog is struggling with. It is important to pay close attention to both your dog's behavior and your own training methods in order to make the most appropriate adjustments for your dog.

SLOW-MOTION REPLAY

Consider using video recording to help you troubleshoot issues. Set up a camera to record both the handler and the dog. Make sure you can play this back in slow motion so you can pinpoint the moment things start to go wrong. This strategy can also help you assess your own performance as a handler. Look, for instance, for any cues you give that may influence the dog's work. Set up your next training trial in a way that avoids these triggers.

SOLVING FORM AND CONTENT PROBLEMS

Remember: the most basic requirement of a scent identification line-up is that a dog be able to work with the scents involved. Training these skills of subtle scent discrimination should be top priority. After all, it doesn't matter if a dog knows all the rules of performing a line-up or looks good doing it if he lacks confidence or skill in distinguishing scents.

Most of the specific tips in this chapter offer strategies for solving form problems, looking at how to adjust training methods for the best results in the dog's willingness and technique, but it is worth taking a moment to talk specifically about content problems and how to address them. First and foremost, when solving a content problem, beware the Clever Hans effect! Do not physically correct or otherwise influence the dog to do what you want it to do. If you do this, the dog will learn to focus its attention on you rather than on the search task, and may only "find the scent" because it is paying attention to your cues.

Instead, when your dog is struggling to make a match, make it as easy as possible for the dog to find the target scent. This may mean reverting to an earlier or easier step in training or allowing the dog to work with materials or scents that it is more familiar with. This will prevent the dog from associating difficult searches with handler influence by getting him to refocus his attention on the scents as quickly as possible.

When a dog is having content difficulties, the handler should also pay less attention to the dog's correct performance of form elements and/or temporarily reward the dog more quickly than usual until the content problem is resolved.

Problems to Watch For

While we can't predict everything that might go wrong over the course of any one training program, there are a number of common problems that come up again and again. Handlers would be wise to watch for these problems and address them as soon as they come up.

FAILING TO PICK UP SCENT

If your dog is having trouble making a scent match, it may be because he has not picked up the scent well enough from the scent object. Sometimes, a dog won't pick up the scent well enough because he does not enjoy the manner in which he is made to smell the object. Often, handlers will hold the dog's snout and place it in front of the scent object—a very dominant behavior on the part of the handler. While this may be necessary when first teaching a dog to take scent (as mentioned in Chapter 5), it risks causing problems down the line. Ultimately, a dog cannot be forced to smell anything. It is therefore important to stimulate the dog's interest in the scent object and allow him to choose to smell it on his own.

Tips:

- Start outdoors, coupling the smelling of an article with a game. For example, after the dog has smelled at an object, use that object in a game of fetch. Later on, hide the object and encourage the dog to locate it by scent.[1] These exercises teach the dog to take scent, and couple the act of taking a scent with that of looking for an object with the same scent, but they do not specifically couple taking a scent with scent identification line-ups.
- Before performing a line-up, hide the scent object to be used in one of three jars. Let the dog locate the jar, and the object, on his own, then reward him for finding it. Then perform the line-up. This helps the dog make the association between the scent object and the scent identification line-up.
- Place the scent object on the ground in front of the platform, and let the dog lie down near it. Ignore the dog. At some point, he will sniff the object by himself. This may take some time. Have patience.

MOVING TOO QUICKLY

Making a scent match between a scent object and scent carrier is easier for the dog if he walks along the platform at a reasonable pace and takes his time to smell each tube. Some dogs do this by nature, but most go too fast and skip some tubes in the line-up. Fast dogs need to be slowed down from the beginning of their training, when the choices they have to make are still fairly simple.

Tips:

- Always take care to have simple choice options available during training sessions.
- Start by having the dog lie down in front of the line-up after having given him the scent. Stroke the dog until he is relaxed.

Very calmly, let him go and ask him to search the platform. It is best to have the dog lying immediately in front of the platform; if he is lying at a distance, he may develop too much speed as he approaches.

- Slow the dog down using a leash. The dog must be used to working on leash before you can do this, to ensure that he does not experience the leash as a punishment. By letting the leash slip gently through your hands, you can regulate the speed of the dog. But be careful: braking the dog continuously may cause the dog to pull, which only increases his speed.
- Slow the dog down by giving the leash a short jerk just before the dog reaches the line-up. This breaks the dog's pace. Again, the dog must already be accustomed to working on leash, and, again, handlers need to be careful: jerking the leash may upset the dog, though this is often only temporary.
- Start the dog perpendicular to a row of scent carriers. This forces him to turn parallel to the row in order to reach the first tube, slowing him down.
- Use psychology! If the high speed of the dog leads him to systematically not smell certain positions in the row, put the target tubes in the positions he systematically misses. For example, position 4 is a common weak position for many dogs: the dog zips past the first four scents, smells positions 5, 6, and 7 well, then turns and smells positions 3, 2, and 1. To counteract this, place the matching scent in position 4 for a few trials. This method works well in combination with a physical slowing down and immediate reward.

FAILING TO BEGIN AT POSITION 1

Both a steady pace on the platform and a systematic approach to smelling every scent tube facilitate the choice the dog has to make. Some of the same techniques used to slow a dog down can be used to have him start at the correct position, with some additional techniques.

Tips:

- Let the dog lie down before allowing him to approach the tubes in the line-up. Stroke him to have him relax, then very calmly let him go.
- If a dog is used to working on a leash, give the leash a short jerk as he approaches the line-up.

- Start the dog perpendicular to the row of scent carriers so that he has to turn parallel to the row to reach position 1, making him start neatly.
- Guide the dog by hand to the first position on the platform.
- Have someone else tap the platform near position 1 to focus the dog's attention there.

STOPPING BEFORE THE END OF THE LINE-UP

Some dogs have a tendency to turn before they reach the end of the line-up, often on position 6. This can be the result of prior conditioning, of a rhythm developed earlier in training, or of poor training design. If you often place the target scent at the beginning of the line-up to encourage the dog to start there, you may ultimately lead the dog to expect to find the target scent there.

Tips:
- Place the target tube at the end of the row several times in an easy-choice scenario (e.g., one scented tube and six unscented tubes). Do not help the dog find the target scent; let him figure it out by himself. Avoid placing the target tube at the end of the row too often since this will only train the opposite problem.
- Place the tube in the line-up randomly, but have someone pretend to place it at the end of the line-up while the dog is watching.
- Walk down the line-up with the dog, and have him smell every tube. Do this in all situations, including when the matching tube is in the beginning of the line-up.
- Increase the distance between the handler and the dog so that the handler's presence exerts less pressure on the dog.

LACKING PERSISTENCE IN CHOICE

During training, many handlers reward their dogs quickly, as a quick reward stimulates the learning process. However, a quick reward will not always be possible. Especially later on in training when the handler works double-blind, the time interval between the response of the dog and his reward will necessarily become greater. After a dog has made a choice, the handler has to signal the line-up assistant and wait for a signal back; only then can the reward be given. Dogs must learn to persist in their choice despite this delay. A dog that expects a quick response can experience this time lapse as a signal that his choice is incorrect, and may abandon the choice.

Tips:
- Consciously increase the time between the response of the dog and the first verbal praise by the handler.
- After a dog has made its choice, reward the dog by petting and physically rewarding him near the tube he has chosen, stimulating the dog to stay with his choice.
- If the dog does react to the correct tube but does not stay there, simply take the dog away and put him in his kennel without comment or reward. For some dogs, this works well: it makes them more eager, and this makes them persist in their choice the next time.
- Start working single- and double-blind as quickly as possible.

INABILITY TO HANDLE MISTAKES

A dog must continue to search, even after receiving a verbal correction. If a dog becomes nervous, he will stop searching well because he is primarily paying attention to his handler. It is crucial that basic trust between dog and handler be built up outside of scent identification training, including around verbal correction.

If a dog reacts strongly to verbal corrections, you may consider giving physical corrections instead. For instance, you may use a very thin leash to correct the dog with a small jerk. To do this, the dog must first be trained to work on a leash. This needs to be done in simple line-ups until the dog is completely accustomed to the leash and is not hindered by it in any way. Only then can the leash be used for corrections.

HAVING PREFERRED SCENTS

Sometimes a dog reacts very strongly to the scent of a certain person and keeps returning to this person's scent. Trying to get the dog to ignore this scent in the same line-up will only lead the dog to pay attention to the handler instead of the search. If it is unclear why the dog is reacting to this scent, then it is better to remove this scent from the line-up and to continue without it.

FAILING TO MAKE RECOGNITIONS

There are a number of reasons that dogs fail to make recognitions—some content-based, and some form-based. Identifying exactly what is causing trouble for your dog is important in order to provide an appropriate remedy.

DIFFICULTY MATCHING SCENTS ON DIFFERENT OBJECTS

In general, dogs find it relatively simple to match scents from identical objects—for example, when tubes are used as both the target-scent object and scent carriers. However, the transition to matching different objects—for example, matching a scent on a T-shirt to stainless-steel scent tubes—can be more difficult, and may need to be a training focus.

Tips:
- Combine the target-scent object with a tube scented by the same person, and offer this combination to the dog for the first match.
- Allow the dog to smell a scented tube first, then to smell an object with the same scent. This gives the dog the opportunity to recognize the scent from the tube on the object.
- Select articles that contain metal parts when asking the dog to make a match with steel scent tubes.
- If a dog has neither made a match nor a mistake, give the dog a tube containing the scent he should be looking for. Then give scent from the scent object again and let him make the match in the line-up.
- If a dog has made a match using one of the above tips, keep the article and tubes of this person and use them again after a short while in a new line-up. For this later line-up, present the article alone, without a tube, as the scent object.

DIFFICULTY MATCHING SCENTS FROM NEW OBJECTS

Dogs may also fail to make recognitions when new things, such as completely different, old, or weak scent objects, are suddenly introduced into training routines that have until then followed a standard form.

Tips:
- Use the scents of people the dog is familiar with.
- If a particular target object went especially well and you see the person who scented it on a regular basis, keep the article well packed, collect fresh tubes from this person a while later, and try again with the now-colder target object.
- Collect two scent objects from a scent donor: an ordinary object that the dog will find relatively easy to work with, and a challenge object that the dog will find more difficult. After a successful match with the ordinary object, give the dog the challenge object. Smelling the challenge object is the learning opportunity for the dog, so this needs to be done carefully. Give the dog time to smell and search without putting any stress or pressure on him. Later in the training, the challenge object can be given first, and the ordinary object can be used to fall back on in case of a nonrecognition. But be aware: if one falls back on the ordinary article too quickly, this can become a habit for the dog too!

OTHER RECOGNITION ISSUES

Dogs may also fail to make a match because the handler has accepted and rewarded a nonrecognition (but not mistake) too often, or too elaborately, in training. The dog walks up and down the row, going through the motions, then cheerfully returns to the handler for his reward. If this is the case, walk the line up and down with the dog. The dog will be paying attention to the handler in this scenario, so the choices in the training line-up need to be simple. It may also help to give the dog a time-out in his kennel when he has not made a match. This makes some dogs more eager to work and more willing to make a choice the next time.

If a dog has problems with recognitions but does make correct choices in the end, it is very important to teach the dog to persist in his choice with strong verbal encouragement.

Finally, poor recognitions can be the result of a physical problem. Even the beginning of an infection such as kennel cough can lead to a diminished sense of smell, as can tooth scale and poor breath. If your dog is in heat, or is about to be, this can affect both her sense of smell and her concentration, both of which can be detrimental to her ability to make recognitions. If your dog is male and another dog is in heat nearby, this can also affect concentration.

LACKING SELF-CONFIDENCE

If your dog is pacing nervously up and down the platform, avoiding the line-up, or positioning himself in ways that lets him keep an eye on his handler, this may be a reflection of low self-confidence in the line-up, possibly due to bad experiences on the platform.

It is important to establish the cause of this behavior. Perhaps too much attention has been paid to a form problem while the content was too difficult. In this case, the usual course is to make the content of a line-up easier for the dog in some way. But be careful: if you revert too often to low-difficulty line-ups, this may also cause problems for the dog. The trick is to challenge the dog without disheartening him.

As a handler or a line-up assistant, it is crucial to remember that sheer difficulty of content is not the only reason a dog may lack confidence. Perhaps the line-up has been improperly set up, with misplaced suspect scents or poorly scented carriers. Maybe you, the handler, are having an off day, and are reacting sharply to mistakes, or maybe you're just working with a sensitive dog. In these cases, what appears to be a lack of confidence in the dog may in fact be a problem that lies with you, not the dog.

LACKING MOTIVATION

Scent identification line-ups require dogs to search independently and with great concentration. One cannot force a dog to search this way; the dog must be self-motivated to do so. Coercion only leads to a dog that pays attention to his handler instead of the scents. For a dog to be self-motivated in this way, he has to enjoy the game of scent identification; performing scent identification line-ups with his handler must be his favorite activity. The quality of the dog-and-handler relationship will play a role in this enjoyment. If your dog isn't enjoying a session, it's better to stop for the day than to press on. Be aware, too, that a lack of motivation may be the result of physical problems such as back pain, sore feet, ear infections, being in heat, or being near another dog who is.

If your dog has low motivation, establish its cause, adjust your training to address it, and have patience. If this doesn't work, it may be time for the dog to move on to a different activity. In extreme cases, it's better to stop scent training all together. Some dogs simply prefer other activities, such as agility or obedience.

Part II

Detection Training and Line-ups

7

Introduction to Detection Work

In detection work, the dog is taught to search for one or more learned odors and to indicate it in the right way by adopting a certain behavior or body position. In professional work in policing, customs, and military, drug and explosive detection dogs are of course best known. But dogs are nowadays trained for many search tasks, including searching for currency or electronic storage devices. In recent years, detection work has also become increasingly popular as a dog sport. It is becoming extremely popular among many pet dog owners.

In the early years of detection work, it was assumed and accepted that the dog knew from the beginning what humans expected of him. Trainers and handlers believed that the dog would be instantly interested in any odor they wanted him to be interested in, and that he would concentrate automatically on that odor. They unconsciously thought that detection training was as simple as obedience training—no harder than teaching a dog to sit or lie down. But the work of searching, unlike the simple command-response training required to get a dog to lie down, is the product of a longer, more systematic training.

Training a reliable detector dog requires an incredible amount of repetition. When we begin to imprint a new target odor on a dog, it is not enough to simply expose the dog to the odor, or even to repeat the exposure a few dozen times. Imprinting a new odor requires something more in the neighborhood of 1,000 to 1,500 repetitions. Over the course of these repetitions, you'll need to present the odor to your dog in many different ways, at many different strengths, and alongside or mixed with many different distractor odors.

It is also important to remember that detector dogs have no inherent interest in the item they are searching for. Dogs are opportunists; what they're ultimately searching for is a reward: their favorite toy or treat. The trainer's job is to make sure the dog pays attention to the scent or odor he has been asked to find, and that he only be rewarded in training when he makes a correct alert. Slowly but surely, and by implementing a consistent reward system, your dog will learn which odor (or odors) pay and which do not.

Finally, it's important to note that detection work is not scent identification work. In scent identification, the dog needs, in every trial, to be able to match a never-before-smelled human scent to a sample from the same person, or indicate that no match exists. Detection work is different. Instead of working with novel scents, the scents and odors a detection dog works with are carefully imprinted on him through training. (Tests have shown that dogs can learn and memorize up to about 40 different smells!) Whenever the dog gets a "search" cue from its handler, it will try to find one of the specific target smells it has been trained on.

Still, there is some overlap in how these two skills are trained—notably, the use of line-ups. Part II of this book introduces readers to the basic skills and knowledge of detection work, and how to use line-ups to train and improve your dog's detection ability and begin working double-blind. Line-ups are extremely useful not only for getting your training reps in, but also, as we saw with scent identification, for training dogs to solve increasingly complex problems and for testing dogs on their accuracy and reliability.

The Early History of Detector Dogs

We can surely count early search-and-rescue (SAR) dogs among the first detector dogs in Europe. These dogs searched for human scent in large woods, under rubble, in snow, or under water. The idea of dogs rescuing people from danger speaks to the imagination. The stories of rescues by the monks with their Saint Bernards high in the Alps at the borders of Switzerland and Italy around 1800 are classics. So is the famous painting *Saved* by Sir Edwin Henry Landseer in 1856, showing a Newfoundland dog on a wharf wall with a girl it has just rescued from the sea lying at its feet.

The development of modern SAR dogs occurred at the end of the nineteenth century as Red Cross dogs began to play an important role in searching for battlefield survivors. The German Association for Red Cross Dogs was established in 1890, and the British Army also trained dogs to search for wounded people. Many of this so-called "ambulance dogs" went on missions in Britain and other countries, including a mission during the war in Manchuria from 1904 to 1905.[1]

We begin to see dogs being used to indicate the presence of nonhuman odors a bit later. The first official American bomb detector dogs came into use in the 1940s for the purpose of detecting German mines in North Africa in the Second World War. In 1942, the American military created Dogs for Defense, an organization that trained dogs (many of which were pets whose families volunteered them for military service) for scout, tunnel, and mine detection. These dogs were taught to find buried metallic and nonmetallic mines, trip wires, and booby traps. The dogs were generally trained to alert by sitting one to four paces from the object or location to which they were alerting. After the war, the dogs that survived were returned to their families.[2]

Dog-and-handler teams were thereafter increasingly used by the US military to locate explosives in war zones. In 1950, the 26th Infantry Platoon at Fort Riley, Kansas, trained dogs for the Korean war (though this project ended in 1953). In the 1960s, mine detector dogs were deployed to Vietnam.[3]

Dogs also began to be used in civilian policing contexts, especially for drug detection. In the 1970s, law enforcement agencies all over the world began to use dogs to uncover various illegal substances such as crack cocaine, marijuana, and heroin. Later on, drug detection dogs were trained to detect methamphetamine, ecstasy, and many other drugs, as well.

Around the same time, dogs began to be used to detect accelerants. One British company, Karenswood (International), claims to have begun researching the efficacy of "hydrocarbon detector dogs" as early as 1964. Because of a general lack of interest in Great Britain at that time, the project was initially marketed overseas. However, due to unremitting efforts on the part of England's West Midlands Fire Service, together with sponsorship from the Eagle Star Insurance Company, Karenswood (International) gave Europe its first very first fire investigation dog, Star, in 1996.[4]

In the meantime, research into K9 detection work was going strong in the United States. In 1983, forensic chemist Richard A. Strobel and explosives investigator Robert Noll began experimenting with the use of dogs in fire investigation.[5] Training dogs in accelerant detection proved to be difficult because of the ubiquity of petroleum products, including accelerants, in our everyday environments. In 1984, researchers, trainers, and investigators began having some success with a Labrador Retriever named Nellie. Nellie assisted investigators in locating evidence of arson at fire scenes, establishing that it was, in fact, feasible to train a dog to detect petroleum accelerants.[6] Soon after, the world saw its first operational "arson dog" in 1986: a black Labrador Retriever named Mattie.[7] Both Nellie and Mattie were acquired from guide dog foundations. By 1988, Mattie, at that time called an "accelerant detection canine," had been trained by the Connecticut State Police with assistance from the Bureau of Alcohol, Tobacco and Firearms to alert to the odors of 17 different ignitable liquids. As Ensminger reports, she had been trained to alert to accelerant odors with a sit position, and was rewarded with food.[8]

The US Bureau of Alcohol, Tobacco and Firearms describes Mattie's role in the investigation of a fire in a manufacturing facility in Branford, Connecticut, in the 1980s as follows:

> Prior to scene-overhaul, Mattie and her trainer/handler, Trooper First Class James Butterworth examined all entrances to the building for possible accelerants. With approximately six to twelve inches of debris on top of the concrete floor, Mattie alerted in one area adjacent to an entrance door. This area was cleared and pour patterns were evident under the debris. She further alerted at the still of the door. Samples were taken from these areas. Later that evening, a vehicle was seized from a suspect. Mattie searched the interior of the suspect's car and alerted on the front passenger floor mat. This alert was later corroborated by witnesses who stated that the suspect carried gasoline to the scene of the arson, storing it on the front passenger side floor of his vehicle. The laboratory confirmed gasoline was present on the mat submitted as evidence.[9]

Mattie's work on this case helped convict the suspected arsonist, expanding the investigative fields in which detector dogs could be confidently used.

Detector Dogs Today

In more recent years, the use of canines for explosives, drugs, and human detection, including search-and-rescue operations, has dramatically increased, as has the list of detection tasks for which dogs are now used.

Dogs can be trained to detect almost any scent or odor. The lists below give an incomplete summary of what odors dogs are used to detect today in professional and sporting contexts. In some contexts, dogs are used to detect more than odors. Medical detector dogs, for example, are used to detect disease as well as certain medically relevant behaviors such as seizures and diabetic shock.

PROFESSIONAL DETECTION ODORS

- Accelerants used to start fires
- Alcohol
- Bed bugs (*Cimex lectularius*)
- Flowers, seeds, fruit, and/or food (e.g., for biosecurity at borders)
- Cadaver (corpses)
- Cell phones
- Currency
- Diseases
- Drugs and narcotics
- Electronic storage devices
- Explosives
- Fungi such as *Serpula lacrymans* (dry rot) and other mold traces
- Specific gaseous chemicals
- Diseases such as cancer, COVID-19, malaria, and Parkinson disease.
- Mercury
- Oil leakage
- Ore deposits
- Prohibited substances
- Termites
- Tobacco
- Truffles
- Wood rot

SPORTS/HOBBY DETECTION ODORS

- Parsley
- Basil
- Mint
- Chamomile
- Oregano
- Lavender
- Dill
- Sage
- Chives
- Lemon balm
- Coriander
- Rosemary
- Thyme
- Cloves
- Ginger
- Star anise
- Cinnamon
- Mace
- Nutmeg
- Tea
- Coffee
- Cacao
- Small pieces of a Kong or other toy

Detection Line-up Training Equipment

There are many different gadgets and setups that you can use to imprint odors on your dog and train him in detection work. These include, but are not limited to, search walls, sorting platforms, a variety of boxes with open and closed tops, Teflon pipes, and odor delivery devices. Ultimately, though, the most important training equipment that detection trainers will work with and need to understand is the odors themselves.

Figure 7.1 Commonly used training tools for detection work. Back left, a search wall made of cones; next to it, a search wall of plastic tubes. Right midground, boxes for odor training. Front left, a line-up of plastic odor delivery devices. To the right, the KNPV sorting platform. Front right, a scent wheel.

Figure 7.2 A professional training wall for detection training. The long, wooden wall is full of holes into which jars holding scent or odor can be loaded from the back.

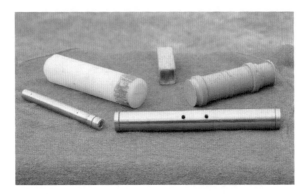

Figure 7.3 Training tools: top left a Teflon pipe, top right a plastic pipe and below metal odor delivery devices.

ODOR DELIVERY DEVICES

Odor delivery devices (ODDs) are small containers typically made of metal or plastic, and are used to safely present odors to dogs in detection line-ups by

Figure 7.4 A homemade ODD made of plastic drainage piping.

Figure 7.5 A commonly used line-up for detection training, using homemade ODDs.

creating a barrier between the dog and the sometimes dangerous substance
it is smelling. ODDs also help prevent the target odor from making direct contact with the place where it is being hidden, contaminating it. Often, depending on the training level of the dog, this kind of contamination can lead the
dog to alert. ODDs are also useful because they are uniform. This means that
every odor will *look* identical, but *smell* different, forcing the dog to use his
nose.

In this book, we use three acronyms to specify what an ODD contains in
any line-up:

- HODD: hot odor delivery device, or an ODD that contains the target odor
- DODD: distraction odor delivery device, or an
  ODD that contains a non-target odor
- BODD: blank odor delivery device, or an ODD
  that does not contain an odor

Training Aids

There are any number of odors that a dog could be trained to detect. Sports trainers and hobbyists, for instance, can train their dogs to detect herbs and spices or the odor of a Kong toy in increasingly small quantities. Professional detection is used for everything from diseases to explosives.

The way in which a scent or odor is collected will depend on what the target substance is, the safety and availability of that substance, the way in which the odor will be presented to the dog, and trainer preference. An odor that has been collected for professional canine detection training purposes is called a *training aid*. Training aids, whether true material, nonpseudo alternatives, or pseudo odors, may be solid, liquid, or gaseous. The training aid's state of matter will affect the dog's ability to detect and locate the source of the odor. Generally, dogs are able to locate the source of the odor if it is solid or liquid, but for gaseous true materials, they may simply be identifying the presence or absence of the odor.[10]

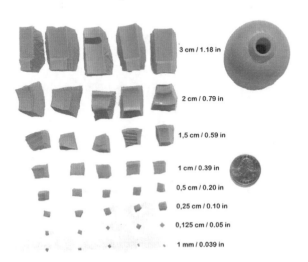

3 cm / 1.18 in

2 cm / 0.79 in

1,5 cm / 0.59 in

1 cm / 0.39 in

0,5 cm / 0.20 in

0,25 cm / 0.10 in

0,125 cm / 0.05 in

1 mm / 0.039 in

Figure 7.6 Training dogs to search for smaller and smaller pieces of Kong toys is a popular activity among hobbyists.

Some training aids are made of *true material*—the actual target substance the dog is being trained to detect. You may also hear this referred to as bulk material, actual material, genuine material, or parent material. Other training aids are made by collecting or suspending the odor of a true material in another substance; these training aids are called *nonpseudo alternatives*. And in some cases, the odors used in a training aid are not collected, but created to mimic the odor of the true material. These are called *pseudo odors.* They are completely synthetic and designed to mimic the odor of the true substance.[11]

Here, as elsewhere in the book, we follow the Organization for Scientific Area Committees' definition of the term *odor:* "volatile chemicals emitted by a substance that are able to be perceived by olfaction," as distinct from the scent emitted by a living human being. For the purposes of this book, the word *substance* here includes anything that is not a living person.[12] K9 detection work is often geared toward detecting odors from substances such as explosives, drugs, cadavers, and insects, and for this reason we use the term *odor* a lot more than *scent* in Part II of this book. It is important to keep in mind, however, that detection work can also be focused on live human scents, such as those specific to certain diseases or bacterial infections.

CHOOSING A TRAINING AID

Can an experienced whiskey drinker sense the difference between a blended and a single-malt whiskey? Does a beef farmer know when he's eating his own, grass-fed hamburger and when he's been given a fast-food alternative? We often see cheap knock-offs being advertised as the "real deal"—but are they really that similar?

The answer is, typically, no—and if humans can make this distinction, you'd better believe dogs can, too. We aren't trying to say that all pseudo odors are "cheap" or that they don't have their place, but we do believe that trainers must take seriously the precision of a good dog's sense of smell. Dogs are extremely good at discriminating scents and odors, even those with very subtle differences. If you do a really good job imprinting a pseudo odor on a dog, that dog will not only be able to distinguish between pseudo odors and the true material, but will be able to pick out the specific brand of pseudo odor he was trained on.

Training a dog on true materials is generally considered best practice, and tends to produce the best result in your dogs.[13] This is because, as Simon et al. note, "pseudos make significant changes to the original odor profile [and] may not provide the same volatiles as the true material, or they may alter volatile ratios."[14] Still, there are a number of reasons you may choose a pseudo or nonpseudo alternative over true material. These include availability, security, safety, transportation, storage, and cost issues related to the true materials.

A nonpseudo alternative odor may be used in place of true materials particularly when it may be hazardous for the dog or trainer to be continuously exposed to the true material. Hazardous true materials include explosives, toxic substances (e.g., fentanyl, synthetic cathinones), infectious materials (e.g., viruses, bacteria, diseases), and pests (e.g., bed bugs). Nonpseudo alternatives are made by using very small amounts of the true material or by collecting or containing its odor, thereby creating a safe training aid that actually uses the true target odor. It is important to remember, however, that these training aids do contain materials other than the true material, and these other materials may influence or alter the target odor to different degrees. Make sure you do your homework before selecting your nonpseudo alternative training aids.

Pseudo odors may also have a place in your work, for instance when the target substance you are training your dog to detect is highly regulated and therefore difficult to obtain.[15] In such cases, pseudo odors may be used instead to give K9 teams access to something rather than nothing. But buyer beware: some courts will not accepts detection evidence from dogs trained on pseudo odors, as studies have shown that pseudo odors do not reliably produce dogs capable of detecting target substances.[16]

However, even if you are able to use true materials in your training, you must still take care in your selection of training aids. True-material training aids may be relatively homogenous compared to the wide variety of possible odor profiles that a target substance may have depending, for example, on its age or the way in which it was made or stored. As Simon et al. note, "It is generally accepted that training dogs on the purest form of a substance is the best method for ensuring reliable detection." However, the target substances found in the real world rarely have this level of purity. Simon et al. continue, "Training on a single pure odor has been shown to produce a strong response and subsequent detection to that specific odor while narrowing the tendency to respond to variations of it."[17] Including true materials of different ages, from different sources, and mixed with different substances may improve your dog's performance in a real-world detection situation.

Regardless of the type of training aids you end up using, always train with the final goal in mind: the dog's ability to detect a target substance in the real world.

Handling, Transportation, and Contamination

Because detection work often involves working with hazardous materials, the number one rule of thumb when handling and transporting training aids is safety. Always take appropriate precautions and follow all protocols when dealing with a substance that could be dangerous to you, your dog, or others.

Careful handling of training aids and equipment is also important for successful training. When storing, transporting, and preparing the odors, tools, and devices required for training, always "work clean." This means taking steps to avoid unwanted and unintentional contamination. When your equipment has taken on other odors or when your training aids have cross-contaminated one another, it can be detrimental to the process of imprinting particular scents and odors onto your dog.

Improper storage is a major contamination risk. If different odors are kept in the same safe, placed in a container that contains or has contained another odor, or even transported in the same car together, they may contaminate each other. It is also important to choose the best storage material for your training aids. We prefer glass jars wrapped in mylar bags. Still, know that all storage material will eventually leak; even with the best storage material, it is still important to store different odors separately. Also know that every time you open a lid and use a training aid in a session, there is increased risk of contamination. At best, handling the storage materials will transfer odor molecules onto the outside of the mylar bags and the outside of the glass, which will eventually leak to the inside. You're also at greater risk of contaminating the training aid directly, so working clean from the beginning and maintaining the separation of your training odors is so important—but really difficult.

There is another risk of contamination when working in a line-up or with a scent wheel: the saliva of the dog. When the dog finds and indicates the target odor, many dogs will briefly touch the hide or container with the ODD, leaving their saliva on the surface. Even if they don't touch it physically, the dog's proximity to the target and behavior around it will almost guarantee that more saliva droplets make their way onto the HODD than any of the other ODDs at play. This means that without thorough cleaning, the dog will find the target odor more easily by simply following the odor of its own saliva in subsequent trials. A similar effect occurs during free-run training searches involving multiple dogs. After a few dogs find the target odors, it becomes easier for the other dogs. They simply start following the odor of first dogs. Be aware of this risk, and be sure to clean your materials well and often.

Figure 7.7 When working in a line-up setting always be aware of the possibility of contamination from the dog's saliva.

SIMPLE CLEANING PROCEDURE

In a line-up setting is important to remove dog saliva, human scent, and other unintended scent and odor cues from our ODDs between trials to get the best results from our training. However, because we want to do as many repetitions as possible in a short amount of time, we need simple, easy-to-follow, and effective cleaning protocols that will not cut into our training time too much. If cleaning procedures pause the training too long, we lose the momentum for our dogs.

We find that disinfectant wipes check all of our cleaning protocol boxes. Take out one wipe and use this same wipe to clean all the ODDs. Just wipe down the surface of each ODD, one after the other. In terms of protocol, there's only one important rule: always make sure you clean the HODD last! This way, you will not contaminate other ODDs with the target odor, which could end up confusing both you and your dog.

HUMAN-SCENT CONTAMINATION

Human scent can also be a contaminant, but this is a bit of a special case and deserves a closer look. When working in a line-up setting, touching an ODD with bare hands is generally not a problem as long you also handle all the other ODDs being used in a line-up in the same way. When done with care, using bare hands to handle ODDs and equipment can have the benefit of not adding latex to the odor profile you're trying to imprint on your dog. When not done carefully, however, directly handling ODDs can cause problems. For example, if your human scent is on the target odor and nowhere else, your dog will easily find this odor by following your scent rather than actually working with the odor. However, if your scent is on all of the ODDs—HODDs, BODDs, and DODDs alike—then it is useless to the dog as a means finding the target odor. The dog will need to sniff out the odor itself and indicate it in order to receive its reward.

Human scent can influence detection training in other ways, too. We have witnessed many police, customs, and military K9 detection exams in which dogs had to search abandoned offices or storage facilities for target odors hidden by the exam administrators. It's not tricky in these scenarios for detection dogs to follow the fresh human tracks to quickly find the target odors. This is not necessarily a problem. For example, if the dog's operational task will be to find contraband hidden in abandoned places, following human scent to the hiding place will be a useful skill. But if your job is finding target odors in crowded areas or places with a lot of coming and going—airports, for example—it will be important for your dog to learn to ignore human-scent distractions rather than to follow them.

Still, there are certainly cases in which we want to avoid introducing human scent onto our training materials—for instance, when we are trying to avoid inadvertently teaching a dog to sniff out our scent rather than the target odor we're trying to imprint. In these cases, we may want to wear gloves when handling our ODDs and other equipment. However, gloves come with their own risks: as already mentioned, if you always use latex gloves to pick up or handle your training aids, you may be accidentally training your dog to search for the odor of latex rather than your target odor. To avoid this, always use clean pliers or tweezers when picking up training aids while wearing gloves.

The best advice we can give is to look at your specific end goal and write an excellent protocol to reach this goal. Different detector dogs will have different operational tasks in different kinds of environments, and their training will need to be tweaked and adapted to those task. Human scent, gloves, clamps, paper bags— work through whatever extra scent or odor cues the dog may encounter in ways that will help the dog succeed at its particular task without getting caught up in distractions. Whatever protocol you end up with, it should teach the dog that the only way to get a reinforcement is to alert to the target odor, and not to other scents or odors around it.

The Right Stuff for the Job

As in scent identification work, it is important to carefully select the dogs, handlers, and teams that will be involved in detection work. While there are no limits on the breeds of dogs that can be trained for this work, it is important to select dogs who are not only up to the task, but also eager to perform. It is also important that handlers in this work clearly understand their roles and have the mental toughness needed for the hard work of training. And, of course, it is critical to develop a strong, trusting working relationship between handler and dog.

Many of the physical and mental qualities of excellent detector dogs and handlers are the same as those of scent detection dogs and handlers. These have already been discussed in Chapter 1. Here, we go over qualities that are more specific to detection work.[18]

PHYSICAL AND MENTAL QUALITIES OF THE DETECTOR DOG

Detector dogs must have an exceptional sense of smell that can flawlessly pick up the smallest clue. They must also have a strong search drive, perseverance, concentration, eagerness to learn, and willingness to work with people. And of course the dog must be physically healthy: he must be free of bone and muscle abnormalities and have a good physique for his future task.

The dog must be extremely eager to learn and eager to be rewarded. This means that the dog should not be difficult to handle or be excessively dominant. He must be good tempered and have a stable character. That is, he must not get nervous in busy environments with challenging and diverse stimuli (think of loud noises, extreme weather conditions, dust, moving objects, unstable or uneven surfaces, and surfaces that differ in height). The dog must be able to relax from high states of excitement reasonably quickly. The dog must also be sociable, approachable, and able to tolerate the presence of other dogs.

On top of all of this, a good detector dog will have excellent hunting, prey, and bring drives. Being able to tap into and develop these drives is especially necessary in the learning phases of detection work, as it will help the dog develop and maintain interest in the work.

By hunting drive, we mean the characteristic, intrinsic desire in dogs to scent for game, to chase it on sight, and ultimately to catch it. This drive includes natural behaviors like searching and tracking. The prey drive is very similar to the hunting drive: it is the drive to not only chase down prey, but to catch and kill it. With the exception of hunting dogs, most dogs are no longer taught to chase wild animals, and the prey drive is now expressed most often in chasing, catching, and shaking toys to "death." In canines living in the wild, the bring drive is expressed in a pack context: a wolf picking up its killed prey, or parts of it, and bringing it to the rest of the pack.

These drives and behaviors form a chain that allows wild dogs to secure their food. The modern dog is typically not burdened with the same need to find food, but these drives are still present as residual traits to greater or lesser extents. For the domesticated dog, however, these residual drives no longer form a chain, but can exist independently of one another. For example, the hunting drive can be present without the prey drive, and the bring drive can have nothing to do with food. The three main drives can then be used to train the dog in other tasks by replacing prey with a toy, stick, ball, or, for Greyhounds for example, a piece of rabbit skin. With its natural canine drives and some focused training, a dog can be trained to pick up and bring any object to the handler; this is usually called retrieving. In detection, the bring drive is used to train the dog to alert—that is, not to bring what he's found to the handler, but to tell the handler that he's found something by performing a specific behavior.

For a dog to be successful in detection work, these drives must be abundantly present. We need a dog with a veritable passion for hunting, catching, and bringing, as these drives form the foundation of detection work. High drives will give a dog the perseverance necessary to continue searching for a target substance, even in the most difficult of circumstances. It will also give it the will to dig, jump, and bite in order to reach the strongest source of an odor—an asset in many detection contexts. In some domesticated dogs, these drives can be extremely low. It is imperative that detector dogs be carefully selected, and that dogs with low or missing drives in any of these areas be weeded out.

Here's a good litmus test for potential detector dogs: watch the dog at play. The dog must be willing to play with and fight for a ball, a rag, or any other toy all day long. He must go completely crazy about his favorite toys. If this character trait is not sufficiently present with toys, one may alternatively see if the dog goes crazy over food. We will talk about determining and using different types of reward systems in Chapter 8.

PHYSICAL AND MENTAL QUALITIES OF THE DETECTOR DOG HANDLER

The K9 detection handler must have specialized knowledge about the odor substances the dog is trained to detect. Most importantly, the handler must be able to work with his dog, together as a team. At the end of the day, a dog will only become as good as his handler permits.

A good knowledge of canine behavior in general, and a better understanding of canine emotional responses in particular, are required reach a high level of detection training. To be a good team member to your dog, you must also understand how your behavior influences your dog. As you and your dog go through the many stages of detection training together, you will come to recognize the meaning behind your dog's many behaviors and reactions.

This learning, as well as the training, takes time and a lot of it. Taking this time is absolutely crucial for success. This is because training a dog to work out the similarities and differences between odors requires long, serious, and purposeful work, not only so the dog knows what is expected of him, but so that you know how to read your dog. When handlers fail to recognize behavioral signals, dogs become confused, which in turn results in handlers becoming frustrated and operating on a hit-and-miss basis. You, the handler, must be able to understand and respond to your dog's reactions quickly and accurately, and understand your dog well enough to explain its behaviors and their meanings to those you're working with. Most modern humans are impatient and don't want to invest the time necessary for detection training. (Remember: imprinting a new odor requires upwards of 1,000 repetitions!) If this kind of time commitment doesn't seem like it's up your alley, you should seriously consider whether detection work is a good fit for you.

One last word: a good handler will not pressure her dog. When a handler uses pressure, successful detection work will not be achieved, ever. A real, friendly understanding between human and dog is an absolute necessity to succeed in this area. The dog has to want from the beginning to respond to the wishes of his handler; it is the handler's responsibility to create an environment in which the dog can want this. Furthermore, the interest of the handler and the dog in one another must grow as far as the differences between them allow. Only in this way can the human and dog successfully complete a task together, with the human lacking the sensitivity of the dog's nose and the dog lacking the human's interest.

8

Reward Systems and Bridge Signals

The basic principles of detection training are twofold: incentive and association. Because the dog is not inherently interested in the specific work of detection or the specific odors he is being trained to detect, we must teach the dog to associate the detection task with a reward or incentive. A consistent reward system will help the dog learn which odors and behaviors pay, and which do not. This chapter breaks down reward systems used in detection training, and how to use bridge signals to help the dog associate his reward with his detection task.

Toy Rewards versus Food Rewards

There are two types of reward systems in detection training: toy rewards and food rewards. This chapter will go over both of these systems.

Both food and toy reward systems are used for professional and sport detection training, and there is some debate over which system gives the best results. Toy rewards are preferred by many, as they stimulate the dog's core drives and allow trainers to turn some of the dog's natural play behaviors, such as searching for a toy, into

Figure 8.1 In detection training, we can choose to use food rewards or, as shown here, toys.

detection duties. However, food rewards may also have their place in some cases.

Some trainers find that food rewards cause problems, especially in professional contexts. One belief is that dogs that are highly motivated by food have low drives. Because the core drives are fundamental to a dog's success in detection training, this would, naturally, be a problem. Another belief is that training dogs with food rewards will result in imprinting a food odor on the dog rather than the target odor you are trying to imprint. In our view, these are valid concerns to have, and should be taken seriously. But neither of these issues mean that food rewards are inherently problematic for professional detection training. First, as discussed in Chapter 7, if your dog has low core drives, it may simply not be the right dog for detection training. Being motivated by food does not, however, mean that a dog is inherently low drive, and using food rewards will not make a high-drive dog into a low-drive dog. Every dog will be unique, and its drives and motivations will be different. Second, toy rewards, as much as food rewards, will have their own particular odors. Whether you use food or a toy, you will still need to carefully train your dog to understand which odors pay and which do not. Consider using food or toy odors in your training as distractors to help solidify this lesson for the dog.

So what reward system should you use? To answer this question, you'll need to really closely look at the dog in front of you. How high are his drives? What motivates him most—food or toys? What type of food or toy? If you have a dog that is highly motivated by food, a food reward system may be the best option regardless. If play motivates your dog most, then toy reward training may make more sense.

TOY REWARDS

The first stages of detection training are all about direct retrieving, then searching and fetching. Toy rewards help stimulate your dog's bring drive and provide a suitable incentive in the form of an object that your dog is able to fetch. Before you begin training specific behaviors with a toy reward, it's very important that your dog has already been trained to let go of the toy on command, and that the dog reliably retrieves the toy when you throw it. The toy that you use should also be something your dog already enjoys working with. You should be able to easily handle this object, and it should be safe for your dog: it should have no sharp edges and be too big for your dog to swallow! Some examples of toys you could use include rolled-up towels, Kong toys, tennis balls, or more specialized equipment such as Teflon or metal pipes.

Toy reward training can be an excellent way to imprint odors on your dog. If you are working with odors that could be dangerous to your dog, such as drugs or explosives, it will be important to use a toy that will create a physical barrier between your dog and the odor, such as a Teflon pipe with a training aid inside. You can also use other toys in a way that will prevent your dog from coming into contact with the substance while still getting your dog to associate the incentive—its toy—with the substance by, for instance, placing the toy near the odor but not directly on top of it.

In all cases, always ensure that your target substance is extremely well packaged and protected against destruction, damage, or loss.

Using a toy reward to imprint odors has four benefits in training:

1. **It acts as a reward.** Rewarding with a training tool at the end of each successful search exercise—finding an odor and giving the correct response—allows your dog to understand that he has completed the command and finished the job. Because the job always ends in a satisfactory way, he becomes receptive to further training.

2. **It acts as a drive stimulator.** At the end of each search, your dog can retrieve his toy reward and should be allowed to play with it. By encouraging your dog's ownership of the object and his play with it, you stimulate his core drives.

3. **It helps your dog build independence.** During training, you need to help your dog develop independence so he is not entirely dependent on you as he searches. Such independence can be developed by hiding a toy reward along with the odor, motivating the dog to search independently with the goal of rewarding himself as quickly as possible.

4. **It helps the handler learn to read the dog.** The toy is a tool that allows you to observe everything your dog does, without interruptions; because the dog is driven to independently find the toy, the handler will be able to observe him from a short distance and gradually learn his body language, identify how he communicates, and understand behaviors to watch for.

FOOD REWARDS

The food reward training method is often used for hobby training of detector dogs, though some trainers also use it in professional contexts.[1] In all contexts, food rewards can be particularly useful at the beginning of training to teach basic skills and condition bridge signals. A food reward is a quick and efficient way of rewarding your dog, allowing you to get in as many repetitions of the early training basics as possible. If you are working with a puppy to train very basic skills, a food reward may make more sense to the puppy, who many not yet see any particular toy to be as valuable as a treat. Once you've established a new behavior with a food reward, you can continue training with that reward or you can replace the food with a toy reward.

When you are working with a dog that is extremely highly motivated by toy rewards, you may also look to food as a way to reward the dog without overstimulating him and taking his mind off the task at hand. By using a slightly lower-value reward during the training session and saving your higher-value reward for the end of the session, you can help your dog stay focused.

The Bridge Signal

Regardless of what reward system you're using, a bridge signal is going to become an important part of your training routine. Bridge signals allow us to create space between ourselves and our dogs, and to increase the time the dog is willing to wait between a target response and a reward.

Figure 8.2 The clicker: one of the most famous and useful devices used as a bridge.

A bridge signal—also called a clear communication signal or secondary reinforcer or marker—is a signal that, when properly trained, tells the dog that reinforcement is on its way. It is, in other words, a bridge between a target behavior and a primary reinforcer such as food or a toy—a tool that helps teach your dog to associate its reward with its job. When the dog is conditioned to the bridge signal, hearing it means "well done; reward is on its way." The dog learns that certain behavior produces a reward and as a result he will show that behavior more often.

USING A BRIDGE SIGNAL IN DETECTION TRAINING

Using a bridge signal in detection training has a number of benefits. By creating space between ourselves and our dogs, we encourage the dog to learn to search independently while still being able to communicate with the dog. This is important for detection work. In area searches, for instance, a dog may be far away from us when it begins to alert. In forensic detection work, it may be important that we don't follow closely after the dog to avoid containing the crime scene

Creating space between you and your dog also avoids disturbing the setting of the search exercise, or inadvertently adding odors or behaviors that will influence the dog's search. This will help the dog focus on searching. And, importantly, reinforcing away from the target odor source gives us more opportunity to shape the dog's behavior. If we bring or throw the reinforcement to the dog, we won't be training the good, focused, long alerts that we can get by standing further away from the dog.

To train a target behavior or imprint a new odor, it's important that the dog is reinforced as soon as possible after it performs the behavior or notices the odor. The bridge signal helps handlers pinpoint the precise moment you want to reinforce. For example, rather than just reinforcing after the dog has found an odor, you can begin to reinforce the dog's perfect, 3-second-long passive alert and focus on a target odor: after exactly 3 seconds of this behavior, you bridge and reinforce. This is particularly true for young or inexperienced dogs that are just beginning detection training: the faster you can reinforce the dog after the desired behavior and bridge signal, the better the conditioning process will go.

Figure 8.3 The bridge signal helps handlers to pinpoint the precise moment the dog's behavior should be reinforced.

As soon the dog is conditioned on a new odor, you can begin to create distance between the position of the target odor and the position where you will reward the dog. If you're using food rewards, this quickly becomes necessary as you don't want to contaminate the target odor and its position with pieces of food that fall from your hand or the dog's mouth while reinforcing the dog. Ultimately detection dogs need to ignore food crumbs during their search, but when you are busy working with a young or inexperienced dog, it's best to start slow. We want to set the animal up for success!

Usually, a bridge signal is given with a whistle, clicker, or ultrasonic signal. It is possible to train a verbal bridge signal—a word that the handler says, such as "yes"—but we don't recommend it. A verbal bridge will always be influenced by your emotion. Your "yes" will sound one way when you're happy, another way when you're down, and yet another way after you've already said it 50 times in a single training session, and this may affect its reinforcing effect on your dog.

There are many ways to condition a bridge, but we love to work with food. The benefit of using food is that it helps you fit in many repetitions in a short period of time. The dog swallows the treat, and we are ready for the next trial. For dogs that are not motivated by food, however, it is also possible to condition a bridge signal with toys. The four-session training schedule below uses food rewards to describe the process of conditioning a clicker bridge signal, but can be adapted to use whatever reward the dog likes the most, and whatever bridge we choose to use.

TRAINING THE BRIDGE SIGNAL

Step 1: Make sure your dog is feeling comfortable. We love to play this conditioning game in the living room or garden. The dog is allowed to walk free without leash. Grab a big bowl with the dog's favorite food and position yourself on a chair. This will interest the dog. Wait a few moments once you have the dog's attention, then sound the clicker and give the dog a piece of food from the bowl. Repeat this every 2 to 5 seconds for a session of 2 minutes. After these 2 minutes, give the dog a break and put the bowl of food away.

Figure 8.4 Present the target odor to your dog in a cup. As soon as the dog sniffs, bridge and reinforce.

Step 2: This step is almost the same as step 1, but we extend the time between clicks. Sound the clicker every 5 to 10 seconds and give the dog some food over a period of 2 minutes.

Step 3: Step 3 begins the same way as steps 1 and 2. Sit down with the bowl of food, and make sure your dog is paying attention. Then wait until the dog looks away. At that moment, sound the clicker. If the dog looks back (and he should), give him a piece of food. In our experience, after about 40 to 50 repetitions, the dog will be well conditioned to the sound of the bridge.

Step 4: Once you have a well-conditioned bridge signal, you can begin to use it to imprint an odor. Present a target odor in a cup to the dog. As soon the dog sniffs it, give a bridge signal and a reward.

In the next chapter, we will look at how to apply reward systems and bridges in basic detection training.

9

Basic Detection Training and Line-ups

It's time to look at the nitty-gritty of how to begin training your dog in detection. First, we discuss the process of imprinting your dog with new odors to detect. Then, we look at the concept of alerts, the pros and cons of active and passive alerts, and how to train these behaviors alongside the basics of detection and using line-ups.

Imprinting Odors

When imprinting odors, the basic principles of detection training—incentive and association—must be front of mind. We've already learned different methods of incentivization, and we've seen how to associate incentives with a bridge signal (Chapter 8). Now we will learn how to incentivize your dog to have interest in the specific odors you want him to find.

Dogs generally aren't naturally interested in the odors we want them to detect, so as handlers we must stimulate the dog's emotional desire to achieve this search work. As a training method, we choose to first help the dog learn an odor and develop an interest in it through reinforcement. This can be done by giving the dog food or play in return for his interest. Later on, we turn this interest into a duty to find the trained odor (or odors).

To create the all-important association between an odor and a reward, ensure that every time you give your dog a reward during training, it is closely related to the odor you are training him on. One of the best ways to do this, in our view, is to ensure the dog perceives the odor alongside the reward at an early stage of training. For example, begin by hiding your dog's favorite tennis ball alongside a cache of the target odor so your dog can immediately take his reward upon finding the odor he is searching for. Later on, only hide the odor. If your dog finds the odor, throw the tennis ball from behind your dog, over him, so he can fetch it.

Learning how to find caches in this way will also help your dog focus his passions for searching and retrieving his toy, which is now strongly associated with the odor. This process can also be adapted to food rewards and bridge signaling. It is not, however, the only way to imprint an odor, and it may not be the right way for your dog. Throwing balls over a dog can be risky; if the dog is very enthusiastic, it may increase the chance of injury. Some dogs may also lose focus on the target odor when they notice the trainer is about to throw a toy—they begin to focus backward (toward the trainer) instead of forward (toward the target odor). Always pay attention to your dog's character and choose a method that works best for him.

IMPRINTING MULTIPLE ODORS

Detector dogs can be trained to detect more than one specific odor. While it is possible to train multiple odors simultaneously— and while this is certainly an efficient approach to training—we prefer to introduce our dogs to different odors one at a time. Only when our dog does well with one odor do we begin to train another. When we do begin training another odor, we continue working with the first odor while simultaneously introducing the second.

We find that this step-by-step method is more effective than the all-at-once method. This is because the all-at-once method risks training a dog to recognize a mixed odor profile rather than multiple individual odor profiles. A dog trained this way may have difficulty detecting its trained odors when they are present individually. While it takes more time, the step-by-step method gives you confidence that your dog is able to recognize each trained odor individually.

Canine Body Language and Alerts

On the job, the handler must pay attention to every little change in his dog's behavior over the course of a search, both before and after the dog detects the target odor, and when the dog has located the odor. These changes may be in the quality of the dog's movements, its pace, its posture, and so on. Even subtle changes can be crucial to understanding a search. Handlers must attend to all of the dog's body movements and behaviors, and learn which specific behaviors their dogs use to indicate that they have detected the presence of odor. Handlers will, of course, learn a dog's behaviors over the course of training. However, to really understand a dog's subtle cues, the handler must be thoroughly acquainted with the dog both in training and work contexts and in normal situations such as relaxing at home. This knowledge requires long and close cooperation.

Every dog's behaviors will be unique, but there are a few common signs that many dogs give when they first catch wind of the target odor and begin hunting it in earnest:

- Suddenly changing direction, making a curve, or otherwise deviating from a generally straight line during searching
- Changing search tempo, becoming faster or slower
- Changing attitude, shown through subtle movements of the ears, tail, or small but detectable changes in behavior
- Lifting the head, tilting it in a certain direction, or standing on hind legs and raising the head to smell the air

- Showing interest in a specific area of the search for somewhat longer than other areas
- Standing still, staring at a certain place, or pointing like a hunting dog
- Scratching or biting at a particular spot, often to remove debris
- Being very excited and making intentional movements to bring the handler to a particular area such as walking back and forth between the handler and a particular spot

The behaviors listed above, and any that the handler learns over the course of their training with the dog, are critical information in detection work, as they tell the handler that the dog is near the target. Crucially, however, these behaviors do not necessarily indicate that a dog has actually found the target. For instance, if a dog scratches or paws at an area only a few times, it is likely still orienting itself and hasn't yet found the right place. To clearly distinguish between these orientation behaviors and the dog actually finding an odor's strongest source, we teach detection dogs to alert.

An alert is a specifically trained behavior that a detector dog performs in a search when, and only when, it has found the strongest source of the target odor. There are two broad categories of alert you can choose to train: passive and active. A passive alert may involve a sit, down, or freeze response from the dog, while an active alert involves barking, scratching, digging, biting, or other more hands-on behaviors. In detector dog training, we see both active and passive alerts—so what type of alert should you choose?

As with reward systems, make sure you train an alert that suits your dog's behavior and character. In terms of reliability, neither type of alert is better than the other. If your dog has well-developed drives, and you've done your job in training your dog to associate his reward with his target odor or odors, you can trust the alert. Nonetheless, it's important to carefully consider the pros and cons of different alert styles and the preferences of your dog before selecting the alert you'll train.

FALSE ALERTS

There are many reasons why dogs make these mistakes. Often, it's because the training is too easy, predictable, or repetitive for the dog. If, for instance, you always place many target odors for your dog to find during short, 10-minute searches, your dog will be used to easy searches with many rewards and reinforcements. Such dogs tend to give more false positives in longer searches without any finds because they get frustrated and try to make their handler start a reinforcing process.

False alerts also occur because of mistakes in odor selection and handling. If you always use distractors that are radically different from the target odor, for instance, your dog may give more false alerts on distractor odors that are similar to the target. Or, if handlers aren't working clean enough, contamination can cause false alerts on inadvertently mixed odors and can even interfere with the process of imprinting an odor on your dog, causing false alerts down the road.

Dogs are also keen on avoiding negative consequences. Using negative reinforcements (removing something that the dog enjoys) and positive punishments (introducing something the dog doesn't like) when the dog makes a mistake can cause your dog to be afraid of you or overly stressed, and could even make the dog afraid of the target odor that you are trying to imprint! Ultimately, this will impact the dog's performance: the dog will focus on the handler, watching for signs of incoming trouble. He will use this information, rather than his nose, to guide his work.

The Active Alert

Active alerts often involve scratching in an attempt to penetrate whatever is covering the odor cache (the place that has the highest concentration of the odor he is trying to find). The type of scratching the dog employs should not be confused with orientational scratching, in which the dog scratches debris away to open odor canals and better smell the odor he is searching for. Active-alert scratching is usually more intense and done in an effort to reach the object emitting the odor. This active-alert scratching may be combined with biting at whatever is covering an odor source.

Of course, this scratching and biting can be dangerous for your dog (e.g., contact with a toxic substance or scratching at dangerous or sharp objects) or yourself (e.g., inhaling dangerous materials that are dispersed by the dog's scratching). It is particularly dangerous if your dog is searching for explosives or very toxic drugs like fentanyl. Furthermore, this type of alert inevitably results in property damage, which may spark lawsuits against the dog handler.

If you are working with dangerous substances in training, it is very important to package and hide them well to ensure your dog will not come into direct contact with them. On the job, the situation is different. If you are searching for contraband, it is likely that the substances will be well hidden and difficult for the dog to directly access, though this isn't always the case. It is therefore very important to be extremely well acquainted with your dog's behavior so you can recognize the alert quickly and stop the behavior before the dog makes contact with a dangerous substance.

A less dangerous active alert, but very old fashioned in the professional detection world, is barking. In a well-trained barking alert, the dog will position himself near the odor clue he wants to alert you to and bark repeatedly or continuously without scratching. This type of alert is suitable for dogs that bark easily of their own volition. However, dogs that alert with barking often do so *after* scratching and becoming irritated when they cannot penetrate the cache fast enough. What's more, a barking alert does not always give handlers enough information about where, exactly, a cache is, and the dog must still be trained to point.

If active alerts have the potential to be dangerous, why use them at all? One reason is that some high-drive dogs begin using these behaviors on their own, and it can be very difficult to get them to stop or change the behaviors to something passive, such as a sit or down. Because of this, some trainers prefer active alerts because they find it easier to teach a dog to "catch the prey"—something high-drive dogs want to do naturally—than to sit in front of the "prey" and wait to be rewarded. For the safety of your dog and yourself, however, we recommend training a passive alert whenever possible.

ACTIVE ALERT DETECTION TRAINING

We like to train dogs to display active responses and search for odors by letting them learn through play, then turning the behaviors they have learned this way into duties. For this type of training, we use a Teflon pipe punctured with small holes. Eventually, we place a training aid in this pipe and firmly seal it at both ends. Repeat the training schedule below to train your dog to give an active alert on all sorts of target odors, in all sorts of wrappings and environments.

ACTIVE ALERT DETECTION TRAINING SCHEDULE

Step 1: Start playing fetch with your empty training device. If your dog likes the game and enthusiastically fetches the pipe, begin filling the pipe with a well-packaged odor. Then begin throwing the pipe when and where your dog cannot see it so he'll have to search for it but will not be able to find it right away. While he is searching, say "search" to begin coupling this command to the activity. When he does find it, reward him by playing fetch with another object, such as a ball. He will quickly get the idea that searching and retrieving will result in a

Figure 9.1 Ruud and his dog play fetch with an odor-filled Teflon pipe.

reward, and he will easily learn to find the tube by its odor. Play this game over the course of a few training sessions.

Step 2: Initiate a game of hide and seek with your dog, hiding the pipe in more and more difficult locations each time you play. You will want to have an assistant on hand to make sure your dog cannot see where you've hidden the pipe. In fact, you'll want more than one person around, because you also need to make sure your dog does not simply follow your track to the pipe. Ask a few other people to walk over the terrain and cross your and your assistant's tracks several times. As the game progresses, make the hiding places more and more difficult to uncover, so your dog has to scratch to get the tube out. When your dog has found the pipe, let him retrieve it and reward him with a ball.

Step 3: Train your dog inside buildings using the same pipe and well-packaged target odor. Hide the tube in various locations that are not too difficult for your dog to find and get at. Praise your dog for scratching at hiding places in order find and retrieve the pipe.

Step 4: Change up your search terrain. Train your dog with your pipe and target odor in a variety of different environments. As you progress, bring in more and more distractions. Ensure the hidden pipe is well covered so your dog must work to find and retrieve it.

Step 5: Repeat steps 2 through 4, but now when hiding the tube in the different places, make sure you cover it with different kinds of wrappings (paper, plastic, fabric, metal).

Step 6: Beginning again at step 1, start training your dog to find a second odor. Always begin by pairing the new odor with an odor you have already trained to make it easier for your dog to detect.

Step 6: Now hide the second odor by itself in a new pipe and see if your dog can find this odor in all situations, from step 2 to step 5. Remember to conduct these exercises in various locations, such as houses, basements, and fields.

The Passive Alert

The advantages of the passive alert in K9 detection are obvious, especially in operational contexts. When the dog gives a passive alert, he poses fewer risks to himself and his handler. Passive alerts can also be used safely in searches for people and does not damage private property. Still, some handlers and instructors are somewhat skeptical about the passive alert, believing that it will decrease the intensity of the dog's all-important drives. But when dogs are trained correctly and rewarded the moment they respond to the

Figure 9.2 A passive sit alert at a scent wheel.

Figure 9.3 A passive down alert at a scent wheel.

odor, we have found that dogs really like the passive response in detection.

Depending on the dog and its training, a passive response may involve sitting, standing, or lying down near the strongest source of the target odor. This passive response should also be accompanied by the dog pointing his nose to the spot that has the most concentrated odor. A dog performing a perfect passive alert, whether sitting or lying down, will be completely still and silent. It will stay in this position for a number of seconds.

TRAINING THE PASSIVE ALERT WITH A KONG

A popular activity among hobbyist trainers is training dogs to detect a Kong. This can be a great way to begin training a passive alert in a toy-motivated dog.

First, make the dog crazy about a Kong. Then, take the Kong in your hand and move it back and forth in front of the dog in such a way that he follows your hand. Stop moving the Kong suddenly and raise your hand a bit so the dog will be lured into a sit position. When the dog sits, open your hand and let the dog reach for the Kong. Continue to train this until you can place your hand with the Kong on the ground and the dog will still give you the sit (or down) to open your hand.

Now place the Kong on the ground, 2 m (6.6 ft.) in front of the dog. Let the dog approach the Kong. If he shows a passive alert, give him the Kong (or another toy) and play with him. If he makes a mistake and grabs the Kong, don't play and restart the exercise. Repeat this until the dog can give you a nice passive alert in front of the Kong.

Now you can begin placing the Kong at different heights, on or in different objects, behind objects, out of sight, or break it into increasingly small pieces—the sky's the limit. The goal is to make sure the dog will go directly into a passive alert when he smells the Kong and is close to it.

Figure 9.4 A passive sit alert, with the dog pinpointing the place where the odor is strongest.

Figure 9.5 A passive down alert, with the dog pinpointing the place where the odor is strongest.

Ultimately, your goal will be to stretch your dog's passive alert to between 2 and 5 seconds. The secret to extending the duration of your dog's alert is in how you use your bridge signal and reinforcement; it is a process of shaping. And always remember the golden rule of reinforcement: you get what you reinforce, so make sure that you only bridge for the wanted behavior. We further discuss how to increase the duration of your dog's alert in Chapters 10 and 11.

PASSIVE ALERT DETECTION TRAINING WITH LINE-UPS

The training sequences below are designed to take your dog from the odor imprinting process through to basic searches while training a passive alert. The sequences show variations using different reward systems. Both methods use line-ups to teach the dog basic detection skills before moving on to other types of searches.

PASSIVE ALERT DETECTION LINE-UP 1: TOY REWARD

Step 1: First, teach your dog to play fetch with a training tool, such as a Teflon pipe, that contains the odor you want to train. This will help to both imprint the odor and get the dog used to, and excited about, the training tool.

Step 2: Set up a line-up. Use boxes or containers large enough to contain a toy—about 30 cm × 30 cm × 20 cm (12 in. × 12 in. × 8 in.). Place one training box containing one odor in a quiet place. Ask your dog to sit in front of the box. Making sure your dog can see what you are doing, insert the toy into the top opening of the box. Allow your dog to go over to the box, but do not let him scratch at it. Instead, give a "sit" command and point at the opening. As soon as your sitting dog presses his nose close to the opening at the top of the box, throw a toy as reward, but make sure the dog does not see you throw it.

Step 3: Once your dog understands that he has to sit in front of the box with the toy, place a second box without odors in a row with the other box. Eventually, you can remove the toy, and have the dog look for the target odor alone. Lead your dog to the boxes, ensuring that the first box he meets is the empty box. To pass from this step to the next one, your dog must correctly proceed to the box with target odor, then give his passive alert. Reward him as you did in step 1.

Step 4: Bring in more empty boxes and regularly change the position of the target box in the line-ups you create. You can use all types of boxes or containers when you create these line-ups.

Step 5: Start training your dog to recognize a second odor, hidden together with the first odor in the box. For each new odor your train, repeat steps 2 through 4, always pairing the new odor with the old odor that is easiest for your dog to detect.

Step 7: Now you can begin training other search contexts. Put a box containing a trained odor in the corner of a room. Let your dog search, sit, and give a passive alert. If he does this correctly, remove the odor from the box and hide it in an accessible spot near where the box

Figure 9.6 Left: The handler allows the dog to watch him put a toy into the box. Center: The box already contains a jar with the target odor in it. Right: In addition to the odor of the toy, the dog now also smells the target odor being imprinted.

Figure 9.7 A passive down alert in a three-container line-up.

had been in earlier trials. Do this with all the odors your dog has been trained on.

Step 8: From this point on, hide your different target odors in increasingly difficult spots—low and high on search walls, in vehicles, in someone's coat, and so on. Also start using distraction odors in your training routine.

Figure 9.8 Left: A dog searches for an odor hidden in a motorized scooter. Center: A Rottweiler finds an odor hidden in the tire of a bicycle. Right: A German Shepherd searches a wall of cones.

PASSIVE ALERT DETECTION LINE-UP 2: FOOD REWARD

Lesson 1

The first lesson uses three identical boxes. These boxes can be quite small as they don't need to contain a toy. As you continue this training schedule, be careful to avoid contamination. Keep track of which box has been used to contain food and, later, your target odor. Use this same box as your target box in lessons 2, 3, and 4.

Step 1: Place an open box containing some food or a few treats on the floor or ground. As soon as the dog sniffs inside the box, sound your clicker and immediately give the dog some food or treats out of your open hand above the box. Repeat this exercise three times and then give the dog an break of at least 15-minutes before moving on to the second step.

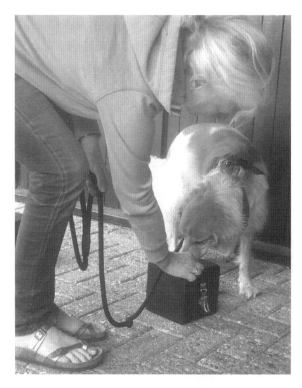

Figure 9.9 A handler rewards her dog directly above the line-up box.

Step 2: Now show the dog a closed box on the floor with a small opening at the top and some food inside. If the dog sniffs the opening at the top of the box, click and immediately give the dog some treats out of your open hand positioned directly above the box. Repeat this exercise three times and then give the dog a break of at least 30 minutes before you go to step 3. These breaks are very important; they allow the dog to think through the exercise and process what has just been learned.

Step 3: Make a line-up of three closed boxes (like the one used in step 2) on the floor, about 1 m (3.3 ft.) from each other. One box has food in it, and the other two are empty. To begin, position the box with food in it at the beginning of the line-up, in position 1. If the dog sniffs the box, reward it as you did in step 2. If the dog was successful, place the food box in position 2, and have the dog investigate the first box, then the second. If successful again, place the box in position 3 and repeat. This makes a total of three repetitions.

If the dog didn't initially sniff the box in the position 1, place the box with the food in position 1 but about 2 m (6.6 ft.) in front of the other two boxes and try again. It is important, however, that you don't repeat these steps too often. Pay attention to the concentration of the dog: he should remain interested in the training. If he is bored or distracted, give him a break before beginning again.

Lesson 2

For this lesson, use the same three boxes from lesson 1, and add another, identical box.

Step 1: Make a row with four closed boxes, one of them with food or treats. This is a repetition of the step 3 in lesson 1, but with one more box. Once complete, give the dog a short break of at least five minutes.

Step 2: Add a good amount of the odor you want to train to the box with the food. Place this box in the first position in the row. If the dog reacts correctly (gives a passive response without your prompting), even if only for a short time, click and reward the dog out of your open hand positioned above the box, then give the dog a break of at least 5 minutes.

Step 3: Repeat step 2 several times, placing the target box at different places in the row. Reduce the amount of food or treat inside the box with each repetition.

Lesson 3

Step 1: Use four identical boxes. In your target box, have only a very small amount of food and a good amount of your target odor. This is otherwise a repetition of step 3 in lesson 2. Have a short break for the dog.

Figure 9.10 Top: A dog searches a line-up of three black boxes. Resi starts her dog at the first box in the row. In this case, this is the box with the training odor and food in it. Bottom: When the dog sniffs the box, Resi presses the clicker and immediately gives the dog a treat, with her hand positioned above the box.

Figure 9.11 As soon as the dog takes a passive response position, immediately give a click and a treat with your hand above the box.

Figure 9.12 A dog correctly puts his nose into the line-up box.

Step 2: Take all the food out of the box so the box is only filled with the odor you want to train. Place this box in the first position of the row. If the dog reacts correctly, click and reward the dog out of your open hand positioned above the box. After a few repetitions, give the dog a break.

Step 3: Repeat step 2 several times, placing the target box in different positions in the row. Make sure you give a fast click when the dog correctly puts his nose in the opening of the box, and a quick reward when the dog alerts on the scented box, even if the alert was very short.

LESSON 4

Step 1: Use four identical boxes. Your target box now only contains the target odor you are training. Step 1 is a repetition of step 3 from lesson 3, but you will be changing the position of the target with each repetition. In this step, you can also begin to work on integrating a correct alert. Once the dog has found the scent, wait for him to dog sit down, possibly giving a soft, spoken command, before clicking and rewarding. Repeat this exercise three times. Give the dog a short break.

Step 2: Slowly reduce the amount of odor in the target box or begin to make the box's opening smaller. In this step, also begin to use odor carriers such as gauze, pieces of tissue, and cotton swabs in the box. These odor carriers can be kept in the same glass jar as the target odor. After several repetitions, give the dog a break.

Figure 9.13 A search for an odor hidden in a brick search wall.

Step 3: Fill one of the previously empty boxes with a small amount of a distractor odor. If the dog alerts to the distraction odor, decrease the amount of distraction odor and/or increase the amount of target odor.

Step 1: Repeat step 3 from lesson 4.

Step 2: Begin changing the types of items and containers that appear in your line-up. For instance, instead of a line-up of four boxes, create a line-up of three small plastic cones, a wooden box, and a cardboard box. Place the target odor in one of the cones and the distractor odor in one of the boxes already used for training. This will help you to see whether the dog has also considered the box as part of the training, and is alerting to the temptation odor because it is in a familiar box. If

Figure 9.14 A search for more hidden odors in a search wall made of cones. The handler, on the right, is operating a clicker with her right hand. An instructor, on the left, stands ready to remove the odor from the wall with tweezers after the dog has found an odor.

Figure 9.15 Top: A Malinois finds an odor hidden in the headlight of a bicycle. Bottom: The Malinois finds a second odor hidden in the bicycle's fender, quite close to the first odor.

this is the case, you will have to take some steps back in the training of the odor. The number of steps you will need to repeat will depend on the dog. Don't be afraid to go right back to the start, if necessary.

Step 3: If step 2 goes well, you can begin training on a search wall. Be sure to put the odor in a small plastic tube (e.g., an Eppendorf tube) or small, open metal container; otherwise, you will contaminate the whole search wall with odor.

In subsequent lessons, you can begin using magnetic containers to hide target odors on the frames of bicycles or cars and having the dog search these. You can also gradually begin to have the dog search rooms and buildings. Integrate distraction odors into these routines.

These training schedules should set you and your dog up with a good foundation in detection skills. But perhaps you've noticed that something important is missing? That's right: we're not yet working double-blind!

In Chapter 10, we'll look at how to take your detection training to the next level, and start working double-blind, with the odor recognition test.

10

The Odor Recognition Test

Have you trained your dog to alert on increasingly smaller pieces a Kong? Have you imprinted various odors on your dog? Have you searched that search wall up and down? Are you ready for the next challenge? Then you're ready to start training for an odor recognition test (ORT).

ORTs are a common type of line-up test used by many training organizations to train, assess, and in some cases certify K9 detection skills. ORTs are worked double-blind and help you prove to your commander, researcher, client, colleagues, competitors, and yourself that your dog is ready for the task. Succeeding at an ORT shows that your dog is well imprinted and conditioned on the requested target odors, and that your dog can find those odors even when present in tiny amounts and alongside an array of distraction odors.

ORTs are sometimes used in competitions, but professional handlers should note that they do not train you for the real-life circumstances of detection work, and are not a perfect indicator of whether your dog will be successful in real operations. Unlike the Dutch scent identification protocol we explored in Part I, detection work is usually performed as an area or building search, and not in a neatly organized line-up. Still, the ORT does give K9 teams crucial experience in working double-blind. If a handler cannot work double-blind with her dog, then the dog-and-handler team is not ready for certification, competition, or operational contexts. Believe us: the operational world is always double-blind.

In this chapter, we go over the training methods for ORTs that will help prepare you and your dog for the real thing.

The Importance of Double-Blind Detection Work

Working double-blind constitutes a big step out of many handlers' and instructors' comfort zones. Some will say that it isn't that important—but we think it's absolutely necessary. It allows handlers and instructors to better understand and test the accuracy and reliability of their dogs and teams—and reliability is critical. When an explosives detection dog gives an alert on cargo that's to be transported by air, that cargo will need to be searched, causing costly travel delays. If a narcotics dog alerts at the dashboard of an expensive BMW, that dash needs to be opened up, leading to potential property damage. And when a tobacco dog alerts on a freight truck, the contents of the truck will need to be unloaded and searched—and that means more labor costs and, again, delays. All of these costs and delays highlight the importance of ensuring K9 detection teams are as reliable as possible.

ORTs allow dog teams to demonstrate to their colleagues and superiors that their work is accurate and reliable. If a K9 team can demonstrate their reliability, the value of their work in operational contexts will be worth the associated expenses and delays.

Double-blind detection training will also help develop your own confidence as a handler and create a working relationship between you and your dog that is based in trust. If you don't make this bonding and trust-building in double-blind contexts part of your training, you will encounter problems when your dog senses your lack of confidence in real-world operations. ORTs allow you

Figure 10.1 A dog performs a double-blind search at a crime scene.

to practice working double-blind, assess how well you and your dog work together, and collect reliable data that can be used to objectively track your progress as a team.

THINK, PLAN, DO

It can be intimidating to develop your own training plan, or even to execute a new plan that has been given to you, especially when it's complicated. Whenever we feel stuck, we fall back on the "Think, Plan, Do" sequence, which we learned from animal training experts Marian and Bob Bailey. Initially, this approach will take time, but your training will be better for it.

Think: Consider what you want to achieve. What do you want your dog to teach? Which specific odor? Which amount(s)? What age(s)—fresh or a few hours or days old? Think about how you will have your dog start a search (from a particular position or platform?) and how you will ask it to alert. Consider how you will reinforce your dog and how you will reset after mistakes. Brainstorm all of the different training steps involved, and how they can be met. Finally, think about all of the materials you will need for your task and how to properly handle them.

Plan: Make sure you have all your materials ready. Do you have all of your target odor and distraction odors? Do you have enough of each? Are they in the correct order? Check in with yourself. Are you ready for training today? Do you have all of your materials? Do you know how you will cope with material failure or a sick dog? Make sure you and your team are ready for all of the tasks you will have to complete in training. Are you prepared to collect data on the fly? Do all handlers understand the ORT you will follow and are they happy with the training schedule? Do we need to discuss anything before we can start?

Do: Now we focus on training! Don't waste any time discussing, building training devices, or fiddling with odors. Now we need to use our precious training time in the best possible way: working with the dogs.

Assessing Progress and Successes

There is no one standardized procedure to draw on when training for ORTs as there is for scent identification line-ups (see Chapter 5), so we need to develop our own well-designed training plans that keep our end goals in mind.

Some handlers and trainers don't organize their trainings around specific, well-defined exercises; they prefer to just go with the flow. The problem with this approach, however, is that it becomes difficult to track your success and to know when your dog is ready to be challenged at a new level of difficulty. The best way to objectively see if you are improving in training or not is to collect data. Collecting data requires (1) breaking up your training into sessions and trials; and (2) having solid system in place for collecting data, and a clear idea of what "success" will look like.

SUCCESS CRITERIA AND THE 80% RULE

What "success" looks like will change depending on the dog's experience and exactly what skill you are trying to train. Before starting a trial, we must know exactly what our success criteria will be so that we can appropriately reward the dog, and so that we can correctly code our data sheet. Some examples of possible success criteria in ORT training include:

- Completing a trial in two runs or fewer
- Alerting to the target odor and nothing else
- Alerting for a duration of at least 3 seconds

When the dog does not meet the criteria we have set, we reset—that is, bring the dog back to the start position—and record the trial as a failure.

Now apply the 80% rule, which we described in the introduction to this book. Continue training the same step of a plan from one session to the next until the dog is at least 80% successful. Better, don't move on to the next step until your dog is 80% successful in at least two consecutive sessions.

COLLECTING DATA

During each training session, we collect data. Of course, we want to know how many times and in which trials the dog was successful at its target tasks. We may also record the speed at which the dog completes the exercise, how long the dog persists in its choice, information about false positive and negative alerts, and so on. Among other things, you can also collect data on:

- The quality of the dog's performance
- The handler
- Environmental factors such as distance, temperature, pressure, wind direction, and distractions
- Target and distraction odors, including amount and age

Many handlers don't like to collect data because they think that it's taking too much time. Some find it hard to analyze, and therefore don't see how it can benefit their training. Others use complicated systems to collect their data, which can lead to confusion. Still others don't want to collect data because they are afraid that management will misuse data or use it to assess the work of the handler. All of these issues can be solved with simple, quick, and easy-to-understand data collection, and luckily we have just the thing!

Figure 10.2 Simon collecting data during an actual training session.

We provide examples of data collection sheets in the training plans below, which you can adapt to your own needs. The challenge is to not collect too much data, and to make sure the data you do collect is relevant to your training task. Remember that in detection training, you'll be doing a lot of repetitions—literally thousands of them! So keep it simple. What do you need to collect to have an objective view of the progress required to achieve your goal(s)?

Conditioning the Dog to Work an ORT Line-up

For the ORT, you will be working with training equipment your dog may not have seen before. These include specific types of odor delivery devices (ODDs) and the containers that hold them in the line-up. These containers are sometimes called *targets*, but to avoid confusion between these and target scents and odors, we will call them *ODD containers* or *holders*. Before you start training double-blind for the ORT, you'll need to condition the dog to work with ODDs and ODD containers and to improve the duration of his alert. There are many ways to do this. We describe one approach here.

Figure 10.3 A Dutch Shepherd performs a detection line-up.

Figure 10.4 ODDs, like the metal ones pictured above, come with different sizes of holes and can be easily used in line-ups and scent wheels.

ORT LINE-UP CONDITIONING SCHEDULE

Step 1: Sniff the ODD container

To set up for step 1, use one line-up position and one ODD. Fill this ODD with an already-conditioned odor, with an already-conditioned odor *and* a new odor, or with a new odor and some dog food. This is now your "hot" odor delivery device (HODD). If you are using food to condition this odor, the amount of food in the HODD should be reduced quickly and be completely gone by step 4 at the latest.

Have the dog sit. Place the ODD container on the floor, about one meter in front of the dog. Then slide the HODD into the container in view of the dog. Give the dog some space and time. Dogs are curious animals, and will eventually sniff and explore the line-up container. As soon the dog sniffs the container, bridge and reinforce. A common mistake at this point is waiting too long before giving the bridge in an attempt to push the dog to give more sniffing behavior, more duration, a full passive alert, or whatever. The success criterion at this moment in training is only "sniff the ODD container."

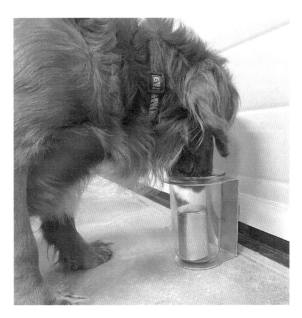

Figure 10.5 As soon as the dog sniffs the ODD container, bridge and reinforce.

Step 2: Sniff the HODD

Now we make the criteria a little bit harder. We repeat step 1, but delay the bridge just a little bit until the dog has put its nose, even a little bit, into the container to sniff the HODD. As soon the nose is close to the HODD, we bridge and reinforce.

You can also begin to add a time criterion: the dog must have its nose near the HODD within 5 seconds of starting. If the dog needs more than 5 seconds, reset and try it again.

Use a simple datasheet to see your progress. Table 10.1 shows a data sheet for one session with 10 trials.

Every time the dog is successful 80% of the time or more, you can make the criteria more difficult. The dog in Table 10.1 scored 70% in its session, so is not ready for the next level. In this case, you would repeat this session with the same success criteria.

Step 3: Two ODD containers, one HODD

Repeat step 2, but this time place another container next to the one you have already used. When the dog is at the start position, he will face not one but two identical ODD containers. In view of the dog,

Figure 10.6 Wait a little bit longer to shape the dog's behavior, getting it to put its nose a little deeper into the ODD container.

Table 10.1 Example "sniff the HODD" datasheet

TRIAL	SUCCESS	FAILURE
1	X	
2	X	
3		X
4	X	
5		X
6		X
7	X	
8	X	
9	X	
10	X	
RATE (%)	70%	30%

Note: Success criterion: Dog has its nose above the HODD within 5 seconds of trial start.

 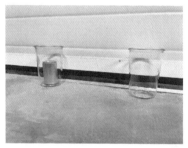

Figure 10.7 Left: One ODD container is empty, and the other is loaded with an HODD. Right: After a few successful trials, change the position of the HODD.

slide an HODD into one of the containers. The other container remains empty. Release the dog and let him search.

In this setup, because the dog has watched the handler place the HODD, he is able to use two sensory systems—his eyes and nose—to find it. When he does, we bridge and reinforce. After a few trials, switch the positions of the containers so the dog doesn't get used to the hot container being in the same place all the time. (To avoid contamination, make sure you move the whole container. Don't just move the HODD from one container to the other.)

To move on to the next step, the dog must be able to find the HODD and keep his nose on it for 2 to 3 seconds at least 80% of the time. Mark successful trials on your data sheet. If the dog keeps his nose on the empty container or keeps switching between containers, reset the dog for 5 seconds before you try again. Mark these trials as failures.

Table 10.2 Example "two ODD containers, one HODD" datasheet

TRIAL	HODD CONTAINER POSITION		SUCCESS	FAILURE
	Left	Right		
1	X			X
2	X			X
3		X	X	
4	X		X	
5		X		X
6	X		X	
7	X			X
8		X	X	
9	X		X	
10	X		X	
RATE (%)			60%	40%

Note: Success criterion: Dog indicates on the HODD for 2–3 seconds.

Keep in mind that we are not working on duration here! We want to make sure that the dog indicates the container with the HODD and skips the empty container. If the dog understands this game, it will be visible in your datasheet!

Step 4: Three ODD containers, one HODD

Step 4 repeats step 3, but with three ODD containers. When the dog is at its start position, it faces three identical containers. Again, slide an HODD into one container in view of the dog. The other containers remain empty. Release the dog and let him search. If the dog puts his nose in the hot container for 2 to 3 seconds, bridge and reinforce. After reinforcing, move all the containers into different positions (left, right, or middle) and start the dog again. Of course, fill in your datasheet! When the dog understands the game, he will ignore or the empty ODD

Figure 10.8 Keep changing the position of the HODD within the line-up.

Table 10.3 Example "three ODD containers, one HODD" datasheet

TRIAL	HODD POSITION			SUCCESS	FAILURE
	Left	Middle	Right		
1	X				X
2		X		X	
3			X	X	
4		X		X	
5	X				X
6			X	X	
7		X		X	
8			X	X	
9			X	X	
10	X			X	
RATE (%)				80%	20%

Note: Success criterion: Dog indicates on the HODD for 2–3 seconds.

containers and quickly focus in on the hot container. When he's 80% successful, you're ready for the next step.

Step 5: Two ODD containers, two ODDs

Now is the moment where the dog begins to learn to trust only his nose. In this step, use one HODD and one blank odor delivery device (BODD). Set up a line-up with two containers. Place the dog in its start position, then load both containers with ODDs in view of the dog. One will have the HODD and the other a BODD. Release the dog and let it search. As soon the dog sniffs the HODD, bridge and reinforce.

Because we changed the game's rules, we need to change the criteria too. Don't wait for a 2 to 3 second response in this step. Bridge quickly! And remember to record your results. For this step, you can use the same data sheet as step 3.

Step 6: Three ODD containers, three ODDs

Set up your line-up as in step 5, but with one more ODD container. Place the dog at the start in front of three ODD containers. Load all containers with ODDs—two with BODDs and one with an HODD. Release the dog and let him search. Now the dog really needs to use his nose! As soon the dog sniffs the HODD, bridge and reinforce. Every trial, change the position of the ODD container with the HODD. Record your results. For this step, you can use the same data sheet as step 4.

Step 7: Introducing distraction odors

As soon the dog understands the concept of searching for and alerting on the HODD and ignoring the two BODDs in the three-odor line-up,

Figure 10.9 Both ODD containers are loaded—one with an HODD, and one with a BODD.

Figure 10.10 All three ODD containers are loaded—one with an HODD, and two with BODDs.

and correctly does this 80% of the time, we are ready to add distraction odor delivery devices (DODDs).

Begin with a three-odor line-up that contains one HODD and two DODDs loaded with the same simple distraction odor. Don't use a difficult distraction like food, a toy, or another odor that is already meaningful to the dog. Use a commonplace but neutral material like paper or plastic.

At first, the dog may take longer to make his choice or even alert on one of the DODDs. This is normal. He has discovered an odor that is different from the BODD, and he's investigating it. Wait until the dog decides to move away from the distraction and bridge as soon the dog sniffs the HODD. Don't wait for the alert. At this stage, our main interest is making sure the dog understands that finding the HODD is the key to getting the reinforcement. Repeat this three times, changing the position of the HODD in each trial.

Now introduce a second distraction odor into the mix to get the dog used to distinguishing the HODD from more than one distraction. Once the dog is able to ignore the DODDs and find the HODD in this setting, you can begin to introduce other distraction odors.

When your dog is consistently able to ignore all DODDs and find the HODD, you can begin waiting for the alert before you reinforce. Move the position of the HODD between trials. When the dog scores 80% or more in this setting, we are ready to add duration into the alerts.

Step 8: Shaping alerts and duration

The rules of the game are clear: the dog knows that finding the HODD and ignoring DODDs will bring reinforcement. Now we can start working on the duration of the dog's response and shaping his alert behavior. This training will focus on a passive alert behavior.

Set up the line-up as you did in step 7. Choose what sort of alert will be the best for your dog. As soon the dog has found the HODD and his nose is in the ODD container, wait a bit longer before you bridge. Waiting longer will usually cause the dog to start to sit or lie down on his own.

When trying to increase the duration of your dog's response, go slowly. If you try to increase your dog's duration of alert by aiming for the longest possible duration every time, you won't be successful. Duration training requires small variations: in one trial, only require a medium duration; in the next, a long one; and in a third, a short one, and so on. To make sure you don't push your dog too much, make a precise protocol for choosing these durations. Before you train, fill in the duration times you want to achieve for each trial and stick to them.

Table 10.4 Example "shaping alerts and duration" datasheet

TRIAL	HODD POSITION			TARGET DURATION (SEC)	SUCCESS	FAILURE
	Left	Middle	Right			
1	X			2		X
2		X		4	X	
3			X	1	X	
4		X		5		X
5	X			2	X	
6			X	1	X	
7		X		6	X	
8			X	2	X	
9			X	3	X	
10	X			1	X	
RATE (%)					80%	20%

Note: Success criterion: Dog indicates on HODD for prescribed duration

Training for the ACT! Odor Recognition Test

Now that your dog is used to working with ORT equipment and has a strong alert, it's time to start training for the test itself. Unlike the KNPV scent identification line-up that we looked at in Part I, there is no one standardized protocol for ORTs—but any good ORT will be transparent, double-blind, and honest. For our purposes in this book, we will look at the ACT! ORT line-up designed by Simon Prins.[1] This ORT tests a single target odor over six trials of eight odors in different line-up positions. In five of the six trials, one of the eight ODDs will be HODDs and the rest will be DODDs. One trial will have a BODD instead of an HODD. This is called a "blank" trial. If you are training your dog to detect multiple odors, you will need to test each odor with its own six-trial ORT.

The official ACT! ORT is performed with an assistant to ensure it is double-blind. However, this doesn't mean you need an assistant to train for the test. The training steps below outline how to train double-blind for the ACT! ORT even when you're on your own.

PREPARING YOUR DATASHEETS

Start by creating straightforward datasheets for your training. Table 10.5 gives an example of a simple datasheet for ORT training that describes the training venue, temperature, and distractions, as well as the target odor and distraction odors used.

Each distraction odor and target odor will be assigned a number, as described below. If you are training with different amounts of target odor, you'll also need to keep track of each HODD using letter labels, also described below. These lists of labels and their odors must be included with your data. Write each odor's label in the "position" column for each trial. In the "runs" column, record the number of times a dog went back and forth over a line-up. In the "result" column, mark whether the trial was a success or not. If the trial wasn't successful, mark whether it ended in a false positive and false negative alert. For false positives, you should record the distraction odor to which the dog alerted. For false negatives, simply mark an *X*. Table 10.6 shows an example of how you might fill out this data sheet over three trials in this training session.

Feel free to build your own data collection system, but keep it simple! As soon as data becomes so complicated that it's not easy

Table 10.5 Blank datasheet for an ACT! training session

Training venue:						Target odor:					
Temperature:						Distraction odors:					
Environmental distractions:											
TRIAL	RUNS	POSITION								RESULT		
		1	2	3	4	5	6	7	8	Success	False +	False –
1												
2												
3												
4												
5												
6												
RATE (%)												

Table 10.6 Example training session datasheet

TRIAL	RUNS	POSITION								RESULT		
		1	2	3	4	5	6	7	8	Success	False +	False –
1	1	16	3	5	11	TA	7	8	13	Yes		
2	2	14	1	17	5	9	15	16	4	No	17	
3	2	TE	11	5	12	8	3	17	9	No		X

to collect and even worse to analyze, we need to go back to the drawing board. Data need to be clear and transparent to be helpful.

PREPARING THE ODDS

The ACT! ORT requires a total of 23 identical, brand new or extremely clean ODDs. These are used to make 5 HODDs, 17 DODDs, and 1 BODD. Number the DODDs 1 to 17 in a place that will not be visible to you while setting up the trials—usually on the bottom. Load the DODDs with their distractor odors; keep a list of the odors associated with each number. Load the HODDs with the target odor. Depending on the dog's level of training, you can vary the amount of target odor in each HODD; record the amount of target odor in each HODD on your list. Label the HODDs in a way that won't be visible to you, using the labels *TA* through *TE*. The *T* is for "target odor." The BODD is labeled in the same way with a *TF*—a false target!

PREPARING THE ODD TABLE

Use tape to divide a table into four squares. We'll use two of these squares now, and the other two later in our trials.

In the bottom left square, place all 17 DODDs filled with different distractions. In the bottom right square, place the 5 HODDs and the BODD. Shuffle the DODDs in their square until you have no idea which number is in which position. Then shuffle the HODDs and BODD in the same way. This shuffling will prepare you to do this training session double-blind.

Figure 10.11 DODDs loaded with different distraction odors and ready for the trial.

Figure 10.12 Labeled ODDs. Left: A DODD with a number label on the bottom. Right: An HODD labeled *TC* on the bottom.

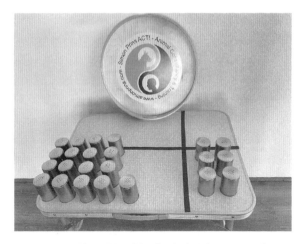

Figure 10.13 The ODD table, divided with tape into four squares.

PREPARING THE LINE-UP

The line-up should include 8 ODD containers in a straight line, each 1 m (3.3 ft.) apart from the next. Place a platform at the beginning of your line-up to provide a clear and consistent start position for the dog.

Figure 10.14 Seven DODDs and one HODD, shuffled on a tray. You should have no idea which is which.

Figure 10.15 Load all containers in the line-up with an ODD. You should have no idea which container holds which ODD.

Put 7 DODDs and 1 HODD on a tray. Shuffle the ODDs on the tray until you have no idea which is which. Because there is also one BODD mixed in with our HODDs, we also won't know if this line-up will be hot or blank. Walk with the tray to the line-up and load all containers with an ODD. This is how we set up a double-blind exercise even when we work alone.

ACT! ORT LINE-UP TRAINING

Trial 1

Place your dog on the starting platform. Give the dog a cue to search. Depending on the dog's level of training, you may walk with the dog on- or off-leash down the line-up or stay at the start position and let the dog work alone. Early on in training, we prefer to walk with the dog on a leash.

Walk a normal pass and make sure the dog sniffs every ODD container. When the dog indicates a container, unlike previous stages of training, we don't immediately bridge and reinforce. This is for two reasons. First, we want to continue our work of building trust, confidence, and alert duration. Second, because we are working double-blind, we have no idea yet if the dog indicated a DODD, a BODD, or an HODD. After a dog has performed a proper alert on an ODD, grab this ODD and check its label to see what it was. Before you set up the next trial, record all of the odor positions in the line-up and the results of the trial in your data sheet.

Figure 10.16 A dog alerts in the line-up.

THE DOG ALERTED ON A DODD OR BODD

So your dog has given a false positive alert. As a handler, it is now essential that you not get frustrated, disappointed, or angry. This is all in the game; mistakes are needed to grow. Just say a simple "no" to the dog, take the ODD out of the line-up position and reset. Early on in training, give the dog a very short time-out (around 5 to 10 seconds), go back to the start, and try the line-up again.

THE DOG ALERTED ON AN HODD

Your dog got it right! Place the HODD back in its container and ask your dog to alert on this ODD again. Remain close to your dog and close to the ODD container. When the dog indicates again, bridge and reinforce. This checking process must feel like an engaging, curious, and nice game for the dog. When the dog indicates, the game starts. It means building up tension: as your hand goes to lift the ODD, check it, and place it back, the dog anticipates its bridge and reward. Play this game in a way that will make your dog love it.

THE DOG GIVES NO ALERT

You've started from the start platform and worked all positions in the line-up, but your dog gave no alert. Bring your dog to the end of the line-up (you may also have a start platform here) and take a short, 5-second break to reset. Then have your dog work back from position 8 to position 1.

If your dog still has made no alert, stay calm—yes, this could be a false negative, but it could also be a perfectly executed blank trial! Place the dog in a secure place, like a kennel, and check all the ODDs. If you find the BODD (labeled *TF*), be happy! Your dog has done well. If you find an HODD, you have a false negative on your hands. Check your list and make a note of what quantity of target odor the dog missed. Work more on this quantity of odor in later training sessions.

Regardless of whether or not this trial was successful, it's time to move on to the next trial.

Subsequent trials

The official ACT! ORT consists of six trials. After each trial, we bring the dog to a safe place like a kennel, your car, or another secure location, then execute the following procedure to set up for the next trial:

1. Record the positions of all ODDs in the line-up.
2. Remove the HODD or BODD from the line-up and place it on the ODD table in the upper right square.
3. Take two DODDs at random from the line-up and place them on the table in the upper left square.
4. Place the remaining five DODDs on the shuffle tray.
5. Take two new DODDs from the bottom left square on the ODD table and place them on the shuffle tray. Clean all the DODDs in the shuffle tray with a cleaning wipe.
6. Take a new HODD (or BODD) from bottom right square on the ODD table and clean it with the same cleaning wipe. Place this ODD on the shuffle tray with the DODDs.

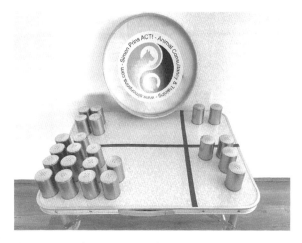

Figure 10.17 The ODD table after two trials, ready for trial 3.

7. Shuffle all the ODDs on the tray, keeping them bottom-down so you can't see how they're marked, until you have no idea which is which.

8. Reload the line-up positions with these ODDs.

9. Collect your dog and start again.

If you need more than three breaks or resets in the same trial, give the dog a more extended break between trials—a few minutes. The exercise is too difficult for the dog. To set your dog up for success, change the trial setting to make it easier. You can get rid of environmental distractions, use more target odor, demand a shorter duration of alert—whatever will help the dog to be successful.

After each six-trial ORT, we clean all the ODD containers in a dishwasher or replace them with new, clean ones before beginning a new ORT.

Training in this way will help you and your dog master the skill of working double-blind in a comfortable and trustworthy manner, will prepare you for success in the official ACT! ORT or another ORT, and will tell you more about the performance and the level of your detection dog. But the ORT isn't the only way to step up your detection training. In Chapter 11, we introduce scent wheels and how they can take your training to another level.

11

Scent Wheel Training

What, you may ask, is a *wheel* doing in a book about *line-up* training? Well, line-ups are certainly crucial tools in detection training, but they can also pose some challenges to dogs and handlers. The most important line-up problem for a lot of handlers is that line-ups have a start and an end. Enthusiastic dogs may completely miss the first few positions in the line-up because they're moving too fast. A bigger problem is when dogs begin to give false positive alerts at the end of a line-up to try to get a reinforcement.

Beyond these problems, there is also the straightforward issue of inefficiency. If we want to reach a high level of reliability and build our dog's odor library, we need to build thousands of repetitions into our training. Loading, unloading, cleaning, reloading, and changing positions of odors in a 10-meter-long line-up with eight positions costs us hundreds of meters of walking and many minutes each trial—and all that work to expose our dog to only eight odors at a time. After working in this way for a while, we became eager to change our training. Enter the scent wheel!

What Is a Scent Wheel?

Scent wheels, also called carousels, address all of these problems. These devices, called *scent wheels* because they were first developed for use in medical contexts involving human scent, have no beginning and no end. They also allow you to do many more repetitions in a short amount of time. A single training session may involve five scent wheels, each with 12 positions. In a single trial, you can ask the dog to discriminate between 60 different scents or odors. In a session of 10 trials, the dog will encounter 600 different or repeating scents or odors. The more repetitions you do, the more efficient and effective your detector dog will be!

Beyond the fact that scent wheels may be the most effective device to imprint odor and improve the work of your detection dog, they will also help you become a better handler. Scent wheels are always worked at a distance from you, meaning that you have little opportunity to influence your dog with your body language or the way you handle the leash. And best of all, they are fun to use for both you and your dog.

There are many different brands of scent wheel to choose from, and you can even make your own. If you are planning to buy a scent

Figure 11.1 Working with a scent wheel is a fun for your dog.

wheel, we recommend Simon Prins's ACT! scent wheels. Over the last 25 years, Simon has built many different scent wheel systems and used many different materials. He started with easy, cheap, and simple devices, and eventually developed the most sophisticated scent wheels available today.

ACT! Scent wheels range from sport to professional. There is even a "sensor and data" version fitted with very sensitive sensors that send the performance data of your dog directly to a phone or tablet. They are designed to train and maintain high-quality detection dogs and to be easy to use for handlers. They are light enough to carry, simple to set up without the use of tools, small enough to transport by car, and quick to tear down, fold up, and store, making it fast and easy to complete a training session.

ACT! wheels are available with 8 or 12 arms, each of which has a horizontal metal ODD holder or vertical glass jar. The benefit of the horizontal setup is that the dog will not leave much of his

Figure 11.2 A scent wheel design that is cheap and can be built fast. This scent wheel is made of plastic cups screwed onto a rotating or wooden base. The base may also be fixed.

Figure 11.3 A trainer sets up her homemade wheel while her dog waits on its starting platform.

Figure 11.4 The ACT! Scent Wheel is a portable system that is light enough to carry, easy to set up and tear down, and offers you the freedom to use vertical and horizontal ODD holders.

own saliva on the ODDs. This is not true of the glass jars; however, these jars make the dog to stick his nose inside, creating a vortex that will make some detection tasks easier, such as detecting very low quantities of odor.

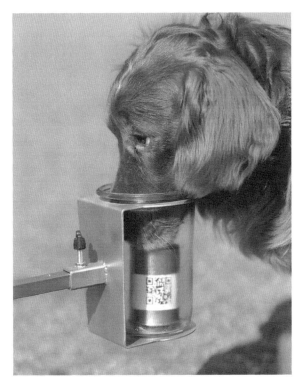

Figure 11.5 A dog working a scent wheel with vertical, glass jars.

Figure 11.6 A dog working a scent wheel with horizontal, metal holders.

Preparing for Scent Wheel Training

Scent wheel training can be added on to any detection training plan to improve your and your dog's skill, confidence, and accuracy. All of the basics of detection discussed in the previous chapters in Part II are important prerequisites to scent wheel training.

BEFORE YOU BEGIN

Before you begin scent wheel training with your dog, make sure you've done a good job with your basic training. The dog must be able to:

1. Recognize the target odor
2. Be conditioned to a bridge signal
3. Be comfortable working with ODDs
4. Give a passive alert like a sit, down, or freeze

We prefer training dogs to use a passive alert with the scent wheel—a sit, freeze, or down. It doesn't matter which of these you use as long as it is clear from your basic training what sort of passive alert you can expect from your dog. This alert will be refined for scent wheel work in the dog's specific scent wheel training. Because you'll be working at a distance from your dog, bridge signals are also used in scent wheel training, and should be well conditioned as described in Chapter 8. Like ORT training, it is important to condition your dog to the equipment used in scent wheel training, such as the specific type of wheel and ODD you will be using. To do this, you can use a method similar to the one described in Chapter 10.

Finally, don't forget about data! The only reliable way to train your dog is to collect and analyze data. We use a very simple datasheet in scent wheel training. Of course, we will keep track of the way you've set up your wheel, as well as place, temperature, and environmental distractions. Write down the target odor and

Table 11.1 Scent wheel training datasheet

TRIAL	BRIDGE	FALSE POSITIVE	CIRCLING TIMES	REMARKS
1	Yes	No	2 x	Success criterion: max 3 times circling allowed before reset
2	No	Tobacco	1 x	
3				
4				
5				
6				
7				
8				
9				
10				

distraction odors, and keep this information with your datasheet. In the sheet itself, we are interested in false positive alerts, and want to keep track of the odors that cause them. Table 11.1 gives an example of the type of scent wheel datasheet we use.

WORKING DOUBLE-BLIND WITH A SCENT WHEEL

As we should know well by now, the best way to build confidence in the dog-and-handler team is to start working double-blind. Scent wheels allow you to work double-blind on your own. By marking the ODDs in a way that will only be visible to you from very close, by spinning the scent wheel, and by following training protocols similar to those used for ACT! ORT training (Chapter 10), you will be able to set up and complete your training sessions double-blind, even if you don't have an assistant.

Lumping and Splitting Your Training

Animal trainers Marian and Bob Bailey taught us two approaches to training that can be applied to any situation: lumping and splitting. When you "lump" training, you just going for it—you put your dog into a new training situation to see how the dog responds and what skills it already has. When you "split" training, you take time to think and make a detailed plan of every step of the training we will do—think, for example, of the "Think, Plan, Do" sequence included in Chapter 10. We think about all the materials that are needed, how to break up training into incremental steps, when to bridge, how to reinforce, what might go wrong, how to handle mistakes—every little detail of each training session.

Both of these approaches to training have benefits and costs. Lumping can save a lot of time, but it also can confuse the dog if done too much or at too high a level of difficulty. Splitting is all about setting your dog up for success, but it can be very time consuming. When used carefully, however, both approaches have their place in detection training.

Below, we give examples of how to use lumping and splitting in your scent wheel training. For simplicity, we describe these processes using an eight-arm wheel, but they can, of course, be easily adapted to a 12-arm wheel.

LUMPING

Lumping can allow you to see where your dog is in terms of skill and ability so you can decide where best to begin your training in a step-by-step training plan. If the dog is not performing at the level required or in the way we expect, immediately stop and switch gears to splitting. Splitting can then help you pinpoint where your dog is having problems, allowing you to develop or adapt a rigorous step-by-step training plan at the right level of difficulty for your dog.

SCENT WHEEL LUMPING

Set up an eight-arm scent wheel with one HODD and seven BODDs. Place the dog in a sit position 2 m (6.6 ft.) in front of the wheel.

Method: Give the wheel a spin—not too fast!—and give the dog a release signal—for instance, "search." Most dogs will go into hunting mode and will approach the wheel simply because they are curious. The goal here is to see if, when the spinning HODD passes the dog's nose, he remembers the odor and starts chasing it. The moment the wheel stops, if the dog indicates, bridge and reinforce.

If you are fully confident and want to take the biggest risk in lumping, you can then fill an eight- or 12-arm scent wheel with 1 HODD and the rest DODDs.

SPLITTING

We prefer to start splitting on a scent wheel with vertical glass jars. We recommend that trainers eventually move to horizontal ODD holders, but starting vertical allows the dog to use not only his nose but also his eyes (seeing the ODD) and his ears (hearing the ODD tinkle against the glass) when beginning to work with a scent wheel. This will help the dog be successful. When working with a vertical scent wheel, however, it is important to think about balance. These glass jars are heavy! When setting up your wheel for the first exercise, you'll use four holders placed evenly around the wheel, at the north, south, east, and west positions.

You can, of course, also begin splitting with a scent wheel with horizontal ODD holders. This will allow the dog to see the ODDs on the wheel, but won't give the added benefit of audible clues. When working with a horizontal scent wheel, you won't have to worry about balance as much, as you won't be dealing with heavy glass. You can therefore begin with only one holder on the wheel and add more as you need them. As you progress, however, it will still be important to add holders in a relatively balanced way (not all on one side, for example) to make sure the wheel does not flip.

The exercises below are described using a vertical scent wheel, but can easily be adapted to a horizontal wheel. When your dog can reliably find the HODD in a particular exercise—that is, when your dog is correct 80% of the time based on your data—he is ready to move on to the next one.

SCENT WHEEL SPLITTING

Exercise 1

For this first exercise, we need four arms: one with an HODD and three that are empty.

Method: Place the dog on the start position about 2 m to 4 m (6.6 ft. to 13.2 ft.) from the scent wheel. In view of the dog, place the HODD in the first glass container. Step back to the start position and release the dog. As soon the dog alerts on the HODD, bridge and reinforce.

Exercises 2 and 3

Again we need four arms evenly spaced around the wheel. In exercise 2, we use one HODD, one BODD, and two empty jars. In exercise 3, we use one HODD, two BODDs, and one empty jar.

Method: Place the dog on the start position. In view of the dog, place the BODD(s) in the first jar(s) the dog will encounter and the HODD in the next holder. Step back to the start position and release the dog. As soon the dog alerts on the HODD, bridge and reinforce.

Exercise 4

Set up the scent wheel as you've done in the previous exercises. This time, you will use one HODD and three BODDs.

Method: Place the dog on the start position. Add the third BODD to the remaining empty glass ODD container in view of the dog. Spin the

Figure 11.7 A scent wheel set up for exercise 1, with four vertical glass jars and one HODD.

Figure 11.8 When working with horizontal ODD holders, it is less important to balance the wheel. This scent wheel is set up for exercise 2, with one HODD and one BODD, but only two arms.

wheel and step back to the start position. Wait for the wheel to stop spinning, then release the dog. As soon as the dog alerts on the HODD, bridge and reinforce.

Exercises 5 and 6

Now we begin adding arms to the wheel and increasing the number of ODDs the dog will encounter. In exercise 5, we use six arms and six ODDs: one HODD and five BODDs. Be sure to position the arms in a way that will balance your wheel. In exercise 6, we use all eight arms and eight ODDs: one HODD and seven BODDs.

Method: These exercises are performed in the same way as exercise 4. If you are working toward using a 12-arm scent wheel, continue with the procedure for exercise 4, slowly building up the number of arms and ODDs you use until all 12 arms hold an ODD: one HODD and 11 BODDs.

Exercise 7: Adding distraction odors

As soon the dog scores 80% in a 10 trial session of exercise 6, it's time to change the rules of the game. Until now, this has been a relatively simple game for the dog: find the ODD that has an odor instead of no odor. Now we can begin adding distraction odors in DODDs to teach him that not all odors pay.

Figure 11.9 A scent wheel set up for exercise 5, with six vertical glass jars, each loaded with an ODD (one HODD and five BODDs).

Figure 11.10 A scent wheel set up for exercise 6, with eight horizontal positions, one HODD, and seven BODDs.

Method: Don't make the mistake of making the first trials of this exercise too complicated. Go a few steps back and use only three arms on your scent wheel, filling it with one HODD and two identical DODDs. (Use a simple, "meaningless" odor that won't be too distracting for the dog, like paper or plastic.) If the dog sniffs or alerts on a DODD, don't panic. Wait for the dog to move on to the HODD. As soon the dog sniffs the HODD, bridge and reinforce. Don't wait for an alert.

When the dog scores 80% or more, you can begin to use two different, simple distraction odors. Again, reinforce quickly when the dog sniffs the HODD, and don't wait for the alert. As the dog progresses, add more and more simple distractions until your scent wheel is full. When the dog is successful in finding the target odor in this setting, you can begin waiting for and shaping the alert. Now is when you can start adding duration!

Increasing complexity

When the dog is 80% successful in exercise 7, it's time to start increasing complexity. Each new session will be a bit more difficult than the previous one. You could begin using weaker target odor, adding more difficult DODDs such as food or toy scents, increasing environmental distraction, allowing less decision time, allowing the dog to only run once or twice around the scent wheel, or changing any parameter that will help your dog meet your specific training goals.

Setting Up for Success, Preparing for Mistakes

If at any time the dog is repeatedly not successful enough to move on to a next step, or if the dog loses interest in an exercise, it's time to change the context and expectation. Be open to going back a step in training, if your dog requires it. Your focus should be on setting up your dog (and yourself!) for success, building motivation and trust along the way.

One way to set a dog up to succeed with scent wheel training, especially when he is struggling, is to load the scent wheel with more HODDs. In this way the dog can quickly earn more reinforcements, and as a handler we like to be able to reinforce fast and often at the beginning of training. For instance, set up an eight-arm scent wheel with vertical jars. Think of these eight jars as being four pairs of two. Depending on the level of the dog and the mistakes he makes, each pair should include either an HODD and a BODD or an HODD and a DODD, giving the dog a 50% chance per pair to alert to the correct odor. Begin by positioning the HODD on the left side of each pair. After a few trial, change this positioning so the dog doesn't learn to alert from memory alone.

And remember: if your dog makes an incorrect alert, do not punish the dog or get frustrated. Let the dog think. If the dog really is convinced that it's a good choice, remove the ODD the dog alerted on from the wheel and reset. This way, the dog will learn what will and will not bring the reinforcement without associating a lack of reinforcement with punishment.

In the next chapter, we take a closer look at specific issues that may come up in your detection and scent wheel training, and how to productively address them with your dog.

12

Troubleshooting Common Problems in Detection

Dogs will make mistakes! Detection dogs will make mistakes! As in any type of training, handlers should expect to encounter challenges and unexpected problems as they and their dogs progress through their detection training. If dog handlers are telling you that their detection dog will never make a mistake, then their training is too simple.

We can think about training challenges in terms of form and content. Briefly, form problems are about technique while content problems are about a dog's issues with the way a line-up or wheel is set up, or the materials used. Before jumping into the common problems in detection training, we recommend reviewing the section on form and content problems in Chapter 6.

Problems to Watch For

Like humans, dogs have different personalities and different learning styles. Every dog will have its own strengths and weaknesses, and while some dogs may experience similar challenges, there is no one-size-fits-all solution that will work every time. Many of the common problems discussed in Chapter 6 in the context of scent identification—as well as the tips and tricks offered to solve them—will be useful to you in detection training, especially if you are working with line-ups. Here, we discuss some of the common problems handlers and dogs encounter in detection work specifically, both in line-ups and with scent wheels, and offer a variety of ways to approach their solutions.

NOT FOCUSING ON THE HODD

Reinforcement issues are often to blame for a dog failing to focus on an HODD, though a number of other factors may be at play, too. If you are struggling to get your dog to focus on an HODD, try some of the following tips.

Tips:

- Try to use a higher-value reinforcer in your next trials, and note whether you see a difference in how your dog works.
- Take a look at your reinforcement procedure. Video yourself or ask a coach to watch you. Focus on your timing, movement, and handling of the reinforcement, and how your dog responds to these. Use this information to make adjustments.
- If you haven't already, condition your dog to a bridge signal instead of handing or throwing him the reinforcement.

Figure 12.1 If a dog is paying more attention to you than to the HODD, it's time to step back and do some focus training.

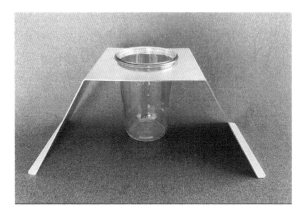

Figure 12.2 Use a single ODD container to work on your focus training.

- Consider the possibility of unintended distractions. Is there an environmental distraction nearby that you as a human can't smell or hear but the dog can?
- Consider the possibility that the target odor has not yet been well imprinted on the dog. If necessary, go back and recondition the odor.
- Make it easier for the dog to recognize the odor of the HODD. This might involve using different or weaker distraction odors and/or increasing the amount of target odor used.
- Change training setup—odor positions, airflow (e.g., by opening a door), distractor odors, environmental distractions, handlers position, and so on. Make notes about whether this makes a difference for your dog.
- Check your data from the last training sessions. Has something changed in your dog's behavior (e.g., dog's time to find the target odor, reaction to distracting odors)?

MOVING TOO QUICKLY

Especially after a few repetitions, most dogs will get the hang of things and start to move fast around the scent wheel or line-up, skipping or not taking enough time to investigate certain odors. Dogs want to get their reinforcement quickly and easily, and if running faster accomplishes that for them, they'll do it. For example, if a target odor is too easy for the dog to find, the dog may run to it as fast as possible for its reinforcement. If you reinforce this behavior, you are indeed reinforcing finding the target odor, but you are also running too quickly.

The following techniques will be helpful for both line-up and wheel settings.

Tips:
- If you're working with a wheel, make sure the wheel is not spinning when the dog works on it. While spinning, the wheel will leave a trail of vapor from the target odor that the dog may pick up and start chasing—and why would the dog put his nose to all those empty ODD holders and blank or distracting ODDs if the hot target is moving in front of him?
- Use a lower amount of target odor to make it more difficult for the dog to detect.
- If working with a scent wheel, use a lower amount of target odor and try one or both of the following:
  › Use vertical holders so the dog will need to stop and put his nose in the holder to get the scent.
  › Use behavior economics. When the dog starts to run, let the dog go two or three times around the scent wheel and then call him back. Give the dog a 2- to 5-second time-out on the start platform and reset. Repeat this a couple of times and you will see that the dog will slow down. He wants to earn his reinforcement, so he will begin to concentrate more and sniff all the ODDs containers. A similar technique can be used in line-ups.
- Add very interesting distractor odors so the dog will be curious about every ODD.
- Work on a leash and slow the dog down, only moving to the next position in the line-up or on the scent wheel when the dog sniffs the ODD container in front of him.

MOVING TOO SLOWLY

If a dog is working too slowly, it may be because you are not sufficiently stimulating his hunting drive. A scent wheel can help here.

Tips:

- Spin the wheel to energize your dog and encourage him to start chasing the odors. A spinning wheel will also ensure that the target odor will pass the dog at some point, so he can pick up on it. As well, the spinning wheel will spread the odor, again encouraging your dog to find its source and chase it down.
- Work with vertical ODD containers because of the way they concentrate odors. If you use a large amount of target odor, it will create an interesting odor source for your dog to explore.

FOCUSING ON THE HANDLER

If your dog is focusing on your instead of the target odor, you'll need to step back to do some focus training. If you're working with a scent wheel, it's best to take a step back from it at this point and work in a line-up setting.

Tips

- Set up a single box with a target odor and place the dog 1 m to 2 m (3.3 ft. to 6.6 ft.) in front of it. Take a curious look at this container while the dog is watching you to stimulate his curiosity. Step away from the box and quickly give the dog a release cue; the dog's curiosity will push him to investigate. When he does, bridge and reinforce.
- Assess your own positioning and behavior. Ensure you are positioned behind the dog and pay attention to your body language and style of speaking. Often, handlers reach for a reinforcement, start talking differently, step toward the dog, or make some other unconscious movement when a dog is near a target odor. All of these are cues for the dog that the reinforcement is coming, and encourage the dog to focus on you instead of the odor.
- Work double-blind as quickly as possible to minimize the way in which your own body language may be influencing your dog.
- Assess your use of the bridge signal. As handlers, we need to be precise about the signal's timing and our own movement. The most important lesson handlers need to learn is first bridge, then move.
- Only give a bridge for the behavior you want. When your dog is at an advanced stage of detection training, for example, we bridge when the dog gives us an alert and is focused on the target odor.

FALSE POSITIVE AND FALSE NEGATIVE ALERTS

Handlers can often address issues with false positive (alerting on the wrong odor) and false negative (not alerting at all when a target odor is present) alerts by changing the training setup.

Tips:

- Make sure you've handled and stored your training aids carefully. Contaminated odors can confuse both you and your dog.
- Work double-blind as quickly as possible to minimize the way in which your own body language may be influencing your dog.
- Check your dog's confidence. If your dog lacks confidence, make the detection problem easier and set him up for success.
- Check your dog's odor recognition skill and work more with different amounts of target odor.
- False negatives may indicate that the dog is going too fast or isn't concentrating enough. Try some of the tips for moving too quickly and not focusing on the HODD.

GIVING AN ACTIVE ALERT WHEN A PASSIVE ALERT IS REQUIRED

We can keep this very simple: you get what you reinforce. When your dog gives an active alert—barking, licking, biting, pawing, or digging—and gets a bridge and reinforcement, you condition those behaviors as part of the dog's alert.

Figure 12.3 If you give a bridge or reward when your dog licks (left) or bites (right) at an HODD, you are conditioning the dog to find the odor, but also the unwanted alert behavior.

Some people find this hard to grasp. They have the idea that the dog understands that they are being rewarded for their behavior up until the bridge signal, not understanding that everything between the bridge and actually getting the reinforcement is conditioned as well. Imagine this: your dog gives a passive alert on a target odor and you give your bridge signal. After the bridge but before the reinforcement, the dog licks the HODD and barks at it. If you then reinforce the dog, it has learned that it needs to indicate, lick, and bark to get a reinforcement.

Handlers also need to be aware of the speed of conditioning. Active alerts can be conditioned with only two or three reinforcements, so it is important to use your data collection to spot the problem as soon as it begins. This isn't a difficult problem to deal with as long as it is identified and dealt with quickly.

Tips:
- Be very clear with yourself on the behavior you want to see, and be careful to only reinforce that behavior.
- Reinforce quickly in the beginning stages of training, and increase the time between the bridge and reinforcement slowly. Try using a remote feeder at the beginning of training so you can bridge and reinforce extremely quickly when the dog gives the desired behavior.
- You can afford to not reinforce if the dog is licking, barking, or pawing at a target odor after you've given a bridge signal if, and only if, conditioning of the wanted behavior is already strong and you've done many successful repetitions. If this is the case, you can simply reset. If not, go back and recondition the desired alert.
- Manipulate the training environment to intercept unwanted behaviors. Set up your ODDs so that if the dog starts to lick them, they fall and the dog is reset. If the dog starts to bark, switch off the light and reset in the dark. If the dog starts to use his paws, set the ODD higher so it's not easy to reach.

LACKING PERSISTENCE IN AN ALERT
Correct use of the bridge signal is crucial to increase the duration of your dog's alert. Again, remember to first bridge, then move. If

you consistently move too quickly to reinforce your dog after an alert, he will never learn to wait for his reward.

Tips:

- Be intentional in your training. Using timers and data to slowly extend the duration of your dog's alert.
- Review the tips for not focusing on the HODD.

Glossary

General Terms

Antecedents: Any cue that precedes a dog's behavior. These can be environmental or handler clues, and can be consciously or unconsciously given.

Clever Hans effect: An animal's ability to produce specific behaviors by responding to humans' conscious and unconscious body language. Named after the famous horse *Kluger Hans*.

Double-blind searches: A line-up or other search in which no one present knows the position of the target scent or odor.

False negative alert or response: The dog gives no alert or response but there is a target odor in the area that the dog has searched.

False positive alert or response: The dog gives an alert or response on something that is not the target odor.

Known searches: A line-up or other search in which the position of the target scent or odor is known to the handler or the dog.

Reward: What the dog is given or allowed to do when it behaves correctly or gives a correct response or alert. In a KNPV-certified dog, the reward is standardized, and is recorded on the dog's certificate. The most common reward in KNPV is being allowed to retrieve the scent-matched stainless-steel tube from the platform. In the context of detection training and ORTs, a reward can be anything the dog enjoys, like food or a toy.

Single-blind searches: A line-up or search in which the handler does not know the position of the target scent or odor, but others present in the search area (e.g., the assistant) do.

Session: A session can be a period of time or a specific amount of trials. For example a session of 5 minutes or 10 trials.

Target scent or odor: A scent or odor that a dog has been trained to detect and/or has been asked to find.

Trial: A single rehearsal of a specific exercise in a session.

Scent Identification Terms

Assistant: A person who is charged with preparing or otherwise assisting in the performance of a scent identification line-up. In an official KNPV scent identification line-up, the assistant must be certified for this task. The assistant throws dice to determine the sequence in which to arrange the scents, sets up the line-up, and terminates the line-up procedure if the dog's behavior or response requires disqualification. If the method calls for it, the assistant may also release rewards for the dog. The assistant co-signs the official report and is named therein.

Certification: The process through which a dog becomes qualified as a scent identification dog. In the Netherlands, this process is defined in article 9 of the Dutch Ministry of the Interior and Ministry of Justice "Regeling politiespeurhonden, 1997" (Police human-scent search dog regulations, 1997). Each certificate is valid for 2 years. The certificate states the kind of scent carriers the dogs works with, the presentation method of these scent carriers, and the dog's specific response behavior.

Cold: Describes scent carriers that are used in a scent identification line-up more than two hours after initial scenting.

Control object: An object given to the control person in a particular line-up to be scented. This object is used to give scent to the dog during the control portion of a check-first line-up. In an official line-up, this object will preferably be made of a material similar to the corpus delicti.

Control person: A designated foil whose scent is used to test the ability of the dog to perform scent identification line-ups. In an official KNPV line-up, this person is recorded in the official report and in the scent identification line-up registration system.

Contamination: Existence of other volatile molecules in a scent trace, which can disrupt identification or even make it impossible.

Corpus delicti: An object or scent sample collected from an object (evidence material) that was taken from the scene of a crime and has very likely been handled by the suspect. In the Netherlands, the corpus delicti must have been accounted for in the line-up's official report and must also be handled according to official guidelines.

Foils: Adults who (as far as is known) are not associated with the suspect's environment and were not involved in the crimes for which the suspect is being investigated. These people's scents are used in the scent identification line-up.

Hot: Scent carriers that are used in a scent identification line-up immediately after scent collecting.

Indication: See *Response*.

Presentation method: In KNPV protocol, the way in which scent carriers must be presented to a dog, as reported on the dog's certificate. The most common presentation method involves a platform with clamps that hold stainless-steel scent carriers.

Response: The KNPV term for the reaction a dog gives when it finds a matching scent. Each dog has its own characteristic response (e.g., bite, scratch, sit, lie down), which is recorded on its certificate. The handler signals the assistant when the dog shows its response behavior.

Scent carrier: The material on which the scents of the suspect, control person, and foils are collected for the line-up. All carriers in a single line-up must be identical and carry no distinctive marks. The most common kind of scent carrier is a scent tube: a small, stainless-steel tube 10 cm (3.9 in.) in length. Other scent carriers are made of aluminum or cloth. The carriers used in a line-up must match the carriers that the dog performing the line-up is certified to use.

Scent sequence: The way in which scents are arranged in any particular line-up. A set of 36 standardized scent sequences are used in scent identification line-ups in the Netherlands.

Scent trace: Scent molecules collected and preserved at the scene of a crime, in a laboratory, or directly from people.

Sorting board: A simple device used to hold scent carriers in a scent identification line-up.

Suspect: A person who is being investigated for a particular crime. In each investigative line-up, there may be only one suspect.

Target object: In a training or competition line-up, an object given to the target person to be scented. It will be used to give scent to the dog. This object is used in the place of a corpus delicti.

Target person: In a training or competition line-up, the person whose scent the dog is being asked to match.

Warm: Describes scent carriers that are used in a scent identification line-up up to two hours after initial scenting.

Detection Terms

Active alert: A type of reaction some dogs give when they finds the strongest source of a target odor. Active alert behaviors include scratching, biting, and continuously barking.

Bridge: A signal used to tell the dog that a reward is coming. The bridge is usually a sound such as a clicker or vocal cue, but may also be a hand signal like a thumbs-up (especially useful for deaf dogs or situations that must maintain quiet).

BODD: A blank odor delivery device, or an ODD that does not contain an odor.

Core drives: The hunting, prey, and bring drives. These drives, or impulses, were developed in wild dogs for the purposes of survival, and remain in many domesticated dogs to different extents. These drives can be used to shape search and retrieval behaviors and are central to developing and maintaining a dog's interest in detection work.

DODD: A distraction odor delivery device, or an ODD that contains a non-target odor.

HODD: A "hot" odor delivery device, or an ODD that contains a target odor.

Nonpseudo alternatives: Training aids that involve true material in their manufacture, but are not entirely made up of true material. Instead, the odor of the true material is collected through processes of dilution, encapsulation, absorption, or extraction.

ODD: Odor delivery devices, or small containers typically made of metal or plastic that are used to safely present odors to dogs in detection line-ups and scent wheels.

ODD container: In the context of detection line-ups and scent wheel training, a jar or other device in which an ODD may be placed or held.

Passive alert: A specific, trained reaction some dogs give when they finds the strongest source of a target odor. Passive alert behaviors include sitting, freezing in place, or lying down near the scent clue. This passive response may be accompanied by the dog pointing his nose toward the place with the most concentrated odor.

Pseudo odors: Training aids that are synthesized to mimic the odor of a true material. Also known as pseudo-odors, pseudos, odor mimics, or simulants.

Search wall: A special wall made of bricks, cones, or other material in which target and distraction odors can be hidden in different places and at different heights.

Training aid: An odor that has been collected or created for canine detection training purposes. Aids can be made by the trainer or handler, by a specialist assistant, or in a laboratory. Training aids may be true material, pseudo odors, or nonpseudo alternatives, depending on how they are collected or made.

True material: The target substance itself. Also known as actual, genuine, bulk, or parental material.

Endnotes

Introduction

1 Our usage of the words scent and odor follow that of the Organization for Scientific Area Committees (OSAC) Dogs and Sensors Subcommittee. OSAC is an organization administered by the US National Institute of Science and Technology (NIST), which replaced the Scientific Working Group for Dogs and Orthogonal Detector Guidelines (SWGDOG), and makes standards and guidelines for the canine detection community. These standards are currently being scientifically validated through the American Academy of Forensic Sciences Standards Board—a process that could serve as the foundation for the certification of detector dog teams. As of 2022, one technical report has been approved. See AAFS Standards Board, *ASB Technical Report 025*.

2 See Gerritsen and Haak, *K9 Professional Tracking*, 30–95.

3 See Pfungst, *Clever Hans*. All information in this section comes from this book.

4 Pfungst, *Clever Hans*, 228.

5 Pfungst, *Clever Hans*, 251.

6 Pfungst, *Clever Hans*, 262.

7 Miklósi et al., "Use of Experimenter-Given Cues."

8 Soproni et al., "Dogs' (Canis familiaris) Responsiveness."

9 Lit, Schweitzer, and Oberbauer, "Handler Beliefs."

1 Introduction to Canine Suspect Identification and Scent Identification Line-ups

1 Schoon and Haak, K9 Suspect Discrimination.

2 AAFS Standards Board, *ASB Technical Report 025*, 35.

3 Curran, Rabin, and Furton, "Analysis of the Uniqueness and Persistence of Human Scent."

4 Vyplelová et al., "Individual Human Odor Fallout."
5 Allen, "The Artificially Scented Ape," 9.
6 Ramotowski, "Composition of Latent Fingerprint Residue."
7 King, Becker, and Markee, "Studies on Olfactory Discrimination in Dogs."
8 King, Becker, and Markee, "Studies on Olfactory Discrimination in Dogs";
   Stewart, Steele, and Downing, "Changes in the Relative Amounts of
   Endogenous and Exogenous Fatty Acids."
9 King, Becker, and Markee, "Studies on Olfactory Discrimination in Dogs";
   Stewart, Steele, and Downing, "Changes in the Relative Amounts of
   Endogenous and Exogenous Fatty Acids."
10 Schmidt, *Polizeihund-Erfolge* (Police dog achievements), 193. Our
   translation.

2 The Early History of Canine Suspect Identification in Europe

1 For an overview of K9 scent identification in American courts, see Prada,
   Curran, and Furton, *Human Scent Evidence*, 11–15; and Ensminger, *Police
   and Military Dogs*, chapter 8. For a European perspective, see Wójcikiewicz,
   Scientific Evidence in Judicial Proceedings.
2 Ensminger, Scent Identification Procedures in the U.S.
3 Schmidt, *Polizeihund-Erfolge* (Police dog achievements), 120–21. Our
   translation.
4 Schmidt, *Polizeihund-Erfolge*, 120–21. Our translation.
5 Schmidt, *Polizeihund-Erfolge*, 126. Our translation.
6 Schmidt, *Polizeihund-Erfolge*, 131–32. Our translation.
7 The cases we describe here are drawn from the memoirs of Dr. van Ledden
   Hulsebosch and Officer Water. See van Ledden Hulsebosch, *Veertig jaren
   speurderswerk* (Forty years of investigative work); and Water, *De grote daden
   van de politiehond Albert* (The great deeds of the police dog Albert).
8 Water, *De grote daden van de politiehond Albert*, 11–12. Our translation.

3 The Development of a Standard Scent Identification Line-up

1 Prada, Curran, and Furton, *Human Scent Evidence*, 10.
2 Much of the history we present in this chapter has been drawn from the
   following references: Rijkspolitie.org, "Historie Korps Rijkspolitie" (History
   of the National Police Corps); van Ledden Hulsebosch, *Veertig jaren
   speurderswerk* (Forty years of investigative work); and Schoon and Massop,
   "Geschiedenis van sorteerproeven door speurhonden" (History of sorting
   tests by sniffer dogs), 964–76.
3 Buytendijk, *De psychologie van den hond* (The psychology of the dog), 87. Our
   translation.
4 Schoon, "The Performance of Dogs."
5 Quoted in van Koppen and Oomkens, "De opkomst en ondergang van de
   geursorteerproef" (The rise and fall of the scent identification line-up test),

467. Our translation. All information in this section is drawn from this source.

4 KNPV Scent Identification Line-ups

1 Ministry of the Interior and Ministry of Justice, *Regeling politiespeurhonden,* 1997 (Police human-scent search dogs regulations, 1997), nos. EA94/U905 and 430262/594/GBJ.

5 Training Dogs in Scent Identification Line-ups

1 KLPD Canine Department, Training of Dogs in Scent Identification Line-ups.

2 Hartman, *Honden leren sorteren en speuren.* Dick Hartman is the pen name of Ruud Haak. More information about this training method can be found in Gerritsen and Haak, *K9 Scent Training.*

6 Troubleshooting Common Problems in Scent Identification

1 This technique is described in Hartman, *Honden leren sorteren en speuren* (Teaching dogs to sort and track).

7 Introduction to Detection Work

1 The history and training of the SAR dogs is not further described here; more information can be found in Gerritsen and Haak, *K9 Search and Rescue.*

2 U.S. Department of Defense, "Four-Legged Fighters"; Kelly, "Poodles Against Hitler."

3 Chriss, "K-9 Units in the Korean War"; Chriss, "War Dogs in Vietnam." See also O'Donnell, *None Came Home.*

4 Karenswood Fire Department, "Fire Investigation Dog"; Karenswood Fire Department, "Our Story."

5 Strobel and Noll, *Pilot Project Arson.*

6 Gialamas, "Enhancement of Fire Scene Investigations."

7 Smith et al., "Pilot Project Arson."

8 Ensminger, *Police and Military Dogs,* 235.

9 US Treasury Department, Bureau of Alcohol, Tobacco and Firearms, and the Connecticut State Police, quoted in Ensminger, *Police and Military Dogs,* 235.

10 Simon et al., "A Review of the Types of Training Aids," 2.

11 Simon et al., "A Review of the Types of Training Aids."

12 AAFS Standards Board, *ASB Technical Report 025,* 28.

13 SWGDOG, General Guidelines.

14 Simon et al., "A Review of the Types of Training Aids," 5.

15 Simon et al., "A Review of the Types of Training Aids," 4.

16 Simon et al., "A Review of the Types of Training Aids," 2–3; Kranz, Strange, and Goodpaster, "Fooling Fido."
17 Simon et al., "A Review of the Types of Training Aids," 3.
18 Farr, Otto, and Szymczak give an excellent overview of dog and team requirements in explosive detection that will also apply to many other areas of detection work. See Farr, Otto, and Szymczak, *Expert Perspectives.*

8 Reward Systems and Bridge Signals

1 Ford K9, "Food for Detection is Bad"; Ford K9, "Question #5: Why Use Food at All in Detection."

10 The Odor Recognition Test

1 More information about ACT!, the ACT! official standard ORT, and the transition from ODD into the real world can be found at https://www.simonprins.com.

Photo Credits

Dog Training Center Oosterhout: 3.4, 4.1, 4.2, 4.4, 5.3, 5.4, 5.5, 5.6, 5.7, 5.8, 7.1, 7.2, 7.4, 7.5, 7.7, 8.1, 9.3, 9.4, 9.5, 9.6, 9.7, 9.8, 9.13. Ruud Haak: 0.1, 0.2, 2.1, 5.1, 7.3, 9.1, 9.2, 9.9, 9.10, 9.11, 9.12, 9.14, 9.15, 9.16, 9.17, 10.1, 10.3, 12.3. Ruud Haak / Korps Landelijke Politie Diensten: 1.1, 1.2, 1.4, 1.5, 1.6, 1.7, 1.8, 1.9, 3.6, 4.3, 4.5, 4.6, 4.7, 4.8, 5.2. *Illustrated Police News*: 2.5. *Onze Hond*: 2.6, 2.7, 3.1, 3.2, 3.3, 3.5. Simon Prins: 8.2, 8.3, 8.4, 10.2, 10.4, 10.5, 10.6, 10.7, 10.8, 10.9, 10.10, 10.11, 10.12, 10.13, 10.14, 10.15, 10.16, 10.17, 10.18, 11.1, 11.2, 11.3, 11.4, 11.5, 11.6, 11.7, 11.8, 11.9, 11.10, 12.1, 12.2. Emma Sheutt: 7.6. Friedo Schmidt, *Verbrecherspur und Polizeihund*: 1.3. Max von Stephanitz, *Der deutsche Schäferhund in Wort und Bild*: 2.2, 2.3, 2.4.

Bibliography

AAFS (American Academy of Forensic Sciences) Standards Board. *ASB Technical Report 025: Crime Scene/Death Investigation—Dogs and Sensors Terms and Definitions.* Gaithersburg, MD: American Academy of Forensic Science Standards, 2017.

Allen, Caroline. "The Artificially Scented Ape: Investigating the Role of Fragrances and Body Odours in Human Interactions." PhD diss., University of Sterling, 2015. http://hdl.handle.net/1893/22599

Brisbin, I. Lehr, Jr., and Steven N. Austad. "Testing the Individual Odour Theory of Canine Olfaction." *Animal Behaviour* 42, no. 1 (1991): 63–69.

Buytendijk, F.J.J. *De psychologie van den hond* (The psychology of the dog). Amsterdam, NL: Kosmos, 1932.

Curran, Allison M., Scott I. Rabin, and K. Furton. "Analysis of the Uniqueness and Persistence of Human Scent." *Forensic Science Communications*, 7, no. 2 (2005): 1-20.

Chriss, Chuck. "K-9 Units in the Korean War." *Olive-Drab.* Accessed July 18, 2022. https://olive-drab.com/od_wardogs_korea.php.

Chriss, Chuck. "War Dogs in Vietnam." *Olive-Drab.* Accessed July 18, 2022. https://olive-drab.com/od_wardogs_vietnam.php.

Derksen, Ton. *Leugens over Louwes: Deventer moordzaak* (Lies about Louwes: Deventer murder case). De Vrije Uitgevers, 2011.

Francis, Vanquilla Shellman. "The Identification of Volatile Organic Compounds From Synthetic Cathinone Derivatives for the Development of Odor Mimic Training Aids." PhD diss., Florida International University, 2017.

Eijk, M.W.v. "Heksenjacht op een zwerver, Onderzoek Oirschotse moord toont duidelijke lekken" (Witch hunt for a bum, Oirschotse murder investigation shows obvious leaks). *Algemeen Dagblad*, February 7, 1970.

Ensminger, John J. *Police and Military Dogs: Criminal Detection, Forensic Evidence, and Judicial Admissibility.* Boca Raton, FL: CRC Press, 2012.

Ensminger, John J. *Scent Identification Procedures in the U.S. Have Different History and Different Procedures from Those Conducted in Europe.* East Lansing, MI: Michigan State University College of Law Animal Legal and Historical Center, 2021. https://www.animallaw.info/article/scent-identification-procedures-us-have-different-history-and-different-procedures-those.

Farr, Brian D., Cynthia M. Otto, and Julia E. Szymczak. "Expert Perspectives on the Performance of Explosive Detection Canines: Operational Requirements." *Animals* 11, no. 7 (2021). https:// doi.org/10.3390/ani11071976.

Ford K9. "Food for Detection is Bad." Uploaded January 17, 2022. YouTube video. https://www.youtube.com/watch?v=RqjDsO1nF1Y.

Ford K9. "Question #5: Why Use Food at All in Detection." Uploaded September 26, 2021. YouTube video. https://www.youtube.com/watch?v=KfSFo5QblIY&t=124s.

Gerritsen, Resi, and Ruud Haak. *K9 Professional Tracking: A Complete Manual for Theory and Training in Clean-Scent Tracking.* Edmonton, AB: Dog Training Press, 2022.

Gerritsen, Resi, and Ruud Haak, *K9 Scent Training: A Manual for Training Your Identification, Tracking and Detection Dog.* Calgary, AB: Dog Training Press, 2015.

Gerritsen, Resi, and Ruud Haak, *K9 Search and Rescue: A Manual for Training the Natural Way.* 2nd ed. Calgary, AB: Dog Training Press, 2014.

Green, Scott C., Mary Ellen Stewart, and Donald T. Downing. "Variation in Sebum Fatty Acid Composition Among Adult Humans." *Journal of Investigative Dermatology* 83, no. 2 (1984): 114–17.

Gialamas, D. M. "Enhancement of fire scene investigations using Accelerant Detection Canines." *Science & Justice* 36, no. 1 (1996): 51–54.

Haan, Bas. *De Deventer moordzaak: Het complot ontrafeld* (The Deventer murder case: The conspiracy unraveled). Nieuw Amsterdam Uitgevers, 2009.

Hartman, D. *Honden leren sorteren en speuren* (Teaching dogs to sort and track). Best, NL: Zuid Boekprodukties, 1991.

Kaldenbach, Jan. *K9 Scent Detection: My Favorite Judge Lives in a Kennel.* Calgary, AB: Detselig, 1998.

Kalmus, Hans. "The Discrimination by the Nose of the Dog of Individual Human Odours and in Particular of the Odours of Twins." *British Journal of Animal Behaviour* 3, no. 1 (1955): 25–31.

Karenswood Fire Department. "Fire Investigation Dog for the Detection of Hydrocarbons." Accessed August 20, 2022. https://www.karenswood.co.uk/fire-investigation-dog-for-the-detection-of-hydrocarbons.

Karenswood Fire Department. "Our Story." Accessed August 20, 2022. https://www.karenswood.co.uk/our-story.

Kelly, Kate. "Poodles Against Hitler: A Canine Unit for World War II." Accessed July 27, 2022. www.americacomesalive.com/poodles-against-hitler.

King, J. Edward, R. Frederick Becker, and J.E. Markee. "Studies on Olfactory Discrimination in Dogs: (3) Ability to Detect Human Odour Trace." *Animal Behaviour* 12, no. 2–3 (1964): 311–15.

KLPD (Korps Landelijke Politie Diensten) Canine Department. *Training of Dogs in Scent Identification Line-ups* [Internal document]. KLPD, November 1999.

Kranz, William D., Nicholas A. Strange, and John V. Goodpaster. "'Fooling Fido'— Chemical and Behavioral Studies of Pseudo-explosive Canine Training Aids." *Anal Bioanalytical Chemstry* 406, no. 30 (2014): 7818–25. https://doi.org/10.1007/s00216-014-8240-7.

Lit, Lisa, Julie B. Schweitzer, and Anita M. Oberbauer. "Handler Beliefs Affect Scent Detection Dog Outcomes." *Animal Cognition* 14, no. 3 (2011): 387–94. https://doi.org/10.1007/s10071-010-0373-2.

Miklósi, Ádám, Rob Polgárdi, Józef Topál, and Vilmos Csányi. "Use of Experimenter-Given Cues in Dogs." *Animal Cognition* 1, no. 2 (1998): 113–21.

Ministry of the Interior and Ministry of Justice. "Regeling politiespeurhonden, 1997" (Police human-scent search dog regulations, 1997). *Staatscourant* (Dutch government gazette) 183, no. 12 (September 17, 1997).

O'Donnell, John E. *None Came Home: The War Dogs of Vietnam.* 1st Book Library, 2001.

Pfungst, Oskar. *Clever Hans (The Horse of Mr. Von Osten): A Contribution to Experimental Animal and Human Psychology.* New York, NY: Holt, Rinehart & Winston, 1911.

Prada, Paola A., Allison M. Curran, and Kenneth G. Furton. *Human Scent Evidence*. Boca Raton, FL: CRC Press, 2014.

Ramotowski, R.S. "Composition of Latent Fingerprint Residue." In *Advances in Fingerprint Technology*, edited by H.C. Lee & R.E. Gaensslen, 63–104. Boca Raton, FL: CRC Press, 2001.

Rechtspraak. *Deventer moordzaak* (The Deventer Murder Case). Accessed August 20, 2022. https://www.rechtspraak.nl/Bekende-rechtszaken/Deventer-moordzaak.

Redactie de Stentor. "Het keukenmes: een moordwapen dat geen moordwapen was" (The kitchen knife: A murder weapon that wasn't a murder weapon). *De Stentor*, September 21, 2019. https://www.destentor.nl/deventer/het-keukenmes-een-moordwapen-dat-geen-moordwapen-was~a9f01a3d/?referrer=https%3A%2F%2Fwww.ecosia.org%2F.

Rijkspolitie.org. "Historie Korps Rijkspolitie" (History of the National Police Corps). Last updated May 10, 2021. https://www.rijkspolitie.org/rp-algemeen/argieven-oud-rpers-2/2099-rijkspolitiegeschiedenis-rijkspolitie-geschiedenis-in-hoofdlijnen-1945-1994.

Schmidt, F. *Polizeihund-Erfolge und Neue Winke für Polizeihund-Führer, -Liebhaber und Behörden* (Police dog achievements and new tips for the police dog handler, -enthusiasts and authorities). Augsburg, DE: Selbstverlag SV, 1911.

Schmidt, F. *Verbrecherspur und Polizeihund* (Criminal trails and police dogs). Augsburg, DE: Selbstverlag SV, 1910.

Schoon, Adee, and Ruud Haak. *K9 Suspect Discrimination: Training and Practicing Scent Identification Line-ups*. Calgary, AB: Detselig, 2002.

Schoon, G.A.A. 1997. "The Performance of Dogs in Identifying Humans by Scent." Thesis, University of Leiden, 1997.

Schoon, G.A.A., and Massop, A.R.L. "Geschiedenis van sorteerproeven door speurhonden." (History of sorting tests by sniffer dogs). *Delikt en Delinkwent* 25, no. 9: 964–76. 1995.

Simon, Alison, Lucia Lazarowski, Melissa Singletary, Jason Barrow, Kelly Van Arsdale, Thomas Angle, Paul Waggoner, and Kathleen Giles. "A Review of the Types of Training Aids Used for Canine Detection Training." *Frontiers Veterinary Science* 7, no. 313 (2020). https://doi.org/10.3389/fvets.2020.00313.

Smith, W., D.C. Lancelot, J. Butterworth, and D.R. Barger. "Pilot Project Arson, Accelerant Detector Dog Program." Paper presented at the Canine Accelerant Detection Training Seminar, Connecticut, August 1988.

Soproni, Krisztina, Ádám Miklósi, József Topál, and Vilmos Csányi. "Dogs' (Canis familiaris) Responsiveness to Human Pointing Gestures." *Journal of Comparative Psychology* 116, no. 1 (2002): 27–34.

Stewart, Mary Ellen, William A. Steele, and Donald T. Downing. "Changes in the Relative Amounts of Endogenous and Exogenous Fatty Acids in the Sebaceous Lipids During Early Adolescence." *Journal of Investigative Dermatology* 92, no. 3 (1989): 371–78.

Strobel, R.A. and R. Noll. *Pilot Project Arson Accelerant Detector Dog Program. The Forensic Science Laboratory's Role*. Paper presented at the Canine Accelerant Detection Training Seminar, Connecticut, August 1988.

SWGDOG (Scientific Working Group on Dog and Orthogonal Detector Guidelines). *SWGDOG SC2 – General Guidelines*. SWGDOG Approved Guidelines. Miami, FL: SWGDOG, 2009.

Thijssen, Wil. "Politie sjoemelde veel langer met geurproeven dan gedacht" (Police cheated much longer with scent line-up tests than thought). *Volkskrant*, November 27, 2019. https://www.volkskrant.nl/cs-bff25f6e.

U.S. Department of Defense. "Four-Legged Fighters." Accessed July 27, 2022. www.defense.gov/Multimedia/Experience/Four-Legged-Fighters/.

van Koppen, P.J., and E.G. Oomkens. "De opkomst en ondergang van de geursorteerproef: Over honden, bewijs en herziening." (The rise and fall of the scent identification line-up test: On dogs, evidence and revision). *Delikt en Delinkwent* 40 (2010): 458–85.

van Ledden Hulsebosch, Christiaan Jacobus. *Veertig jaren speurderswerk* (Forty years of investigative work). Utrecht, NL: Kemink en Zoon N.V., 1945.

von Stephanitz, Max. *Der deutsche Schäferhund in Wort und Bild* (The German Shepherd dog in words and images). Jena: Anton Kampfe, 1923. First published 1901 by Verein für deutsche Schäferhunde.

Vyplelová, Petra, Václav Vokálek, Ludvík Pinc, Zuzana Pacáková, Luděk Bartoš, Milena Santariová, and Zuzana Čapková. "Individual Human Odor Fallout as Detected by Trained Canines." *Forensic Science International* 234 (2014): 13–15.

Water, Jacob. "De grote daden van de politiehond 'Albert'". (The great deeds of the police dog "Albert"). *De Courant: Nieuws van de Dag*, 1948.

Wójcikiewicz, Józef. *Scientific Evidence in Judicial Proceedings*. Kraków, PL: Institute of Forensic Research Publishers, 2000.

About the Authors

Ruud Haak is the author of more than 30 dog books in Dutch and German, and for over 40 years he has been the editor-in-chief of the biggest Dutch dog magazine, *Onze Hond* (Our dog). He was born in 1947 in Amsterdam, the Netherlands. At the age of 13, he was training police dogs at his uncle's security dog training center. When he was 15, he worked after school with his patrol dog (which he trained himself) at the Amsterdam harbor. He later started training his dogs in Schutzhund (IPO-IGP), and he successfully bred and showed German Shepherd and Saint Bernard dogs.

Ruud worked as a social therapist in a government clinic for criminal psychopaths. From his studies in psychology, he became interested in dog behavior and training methods for nose work, especially the tracking dog and the search-and-rescue dog. More recently he has trained drug- and explosive-detector dogs for the Dutch police and the Royal Dutch Airforce. He is also a visiting lecturer at Dutch, German, and Austrian police-dog schools.

In the 1970s, Ruud and his wife, **Dr. Resi Gerritsen**, a psychologist and jurist, attended many courses and symposia with their German Shepherds for Schutzhund, tracking dog, and search-and-rescue dog training in Switzerland, Germany, and Austria.

Ruud Haak with his German Shepherd Yes van Sulieseraad and Malinois Google van het Eldenseveld.

In 1979, they started the Dutch Rescue Dog Organization in the Netherlands. With that unit, they attended many operations responding to earthquakes, gas explosions, and lost persons in wooded or wilderness areas. In 1990, Ruud and Resi moved to Austria, where they were asked by the Austrian Red Cross to select and train operational search-and-rescue and avalanche dogs. They lived for three years at a height of 1800 m (6000 ft.) in the Alps and worked with their dogs in search missions after avalanches.

With their Austrian colleagues, Ruud and Resi developed a new method for training search-and-rescue dogs. Their methods showed the best results after a major earthquake in Armenia (1988), an earthquake in Japan (1995), two major earthquakes in Turkey (1999), and big earthquakes in Algeria and Iran (2003). Ruud and Resi have also demonstrated the success of their unique training methods for tracking dogs as well as search-and-rescue dogs at the Austrian, Czech, Hungarian, and World Championships, where both were the leading champions several times.

Resi Gerritsen with her young German Shepherd Donna
vom Mueller Haus and Malinois Pepper van de Denarius.

Resi and Ruud have held many symposia and master classes
all over the world on their unique training methods, which are
featured in their books:

- *K9 Complete Care: A Manual for Physically and Mentally Healthy Working Dogs*
- *K9 Drug Detection: A Manual for Training and Operations*
- *K9 Explosive and Mine Detection: A Manual for Training and Operations*
- *K9 Investigation Errors and How to Avoid Them*
- *K9 Personal Protection: A Manual for Training Reliable Protection Dogs*
- *K9 Professional Tracking: A Complete Manual for Theory and Training*
- *K9 Scent Training: A Manual for Training Your Identification, Tracking, and Detection Dog*
- *K9 Schutzhund: A Manual for IGP Training through Positive Reinforcement*
- *K9 Search and Rescue: A Manual for Training the Natural Way*
- *K9 Working Breeds: Characteristics and Capabilities*
- *The German Shepherd Dog: A Historical View of the Breed's Development, Prime, and Deterioration*

- *The Labrador Retriever: From Hunting Dog to One of the World's Most Versatile Working Dogs*
- *The Malinois: The History and Development of the Breed in Schutzhund, Detection and Police Work*

With Simon Prins they wrote *K9 Behavior Basics: A Manual for Proven Success in Operational Service Dog Training*, and with Dr. Adee Schoon, Ruud wrote *K9 Suspect Discrimination: Training and Practicing Scent Identification Line-Ups*. All of these books were published by Detselig Enterprises Ltd., Calgary, Canada (now Brush Education Inc.).

Ruud and Resi now live in the Netherlands. They are international judges for the International Rescue Dog Organisation (IRO) and the Fédération Cynologique Internationale (FCI). Ruud and Resi are still successfully training their dogs for search and rescue, detection work, and Schutzhund. You can contact the authors by email at resigerritsen@gmail.com.

Simon Prins is known for introducing operant conditioning to the Police K9 training world. For the last 25 years, he has worked in K9 special operations, skillfully trained dogs for special operations missions, and mastered the art of using robotics and sensors with dogs to perform such tasks successfully. He has titled and trained countless dogs and trainers from special units across the globe, and firmly believes that science can significantly improve our work with animals.

Simon is a speaker, author, innovator, animal trainer, and behaviorist. He started working with hunting dogs in 1989, and is currently working with the Netherlands Police Agency. He joined the police force as one of the youngest patrol dog handlers at the time, and worked with these dogs for several years. In 1996, he was asked to set up a special K9 research and development project. Working with radio-guided camera dogs was one of the many topics of this

Simon Prins with one of the many dogs he has trained for police and military duties using operant conditioning methods.

program. In the years that followed, he started programs for hard-surface tracking, laser-guided attack dogs, and detection dogs for special operations. In 2006, he began training radio-guided dogs equipped with sensors to carry small robots into operations. Simon has also worked in search-and-rescue contexts, selecting and training the first 16 dogs and handlers for the official Dutch search-and-rescue team, the USAR, in 2002.

Over the years, Simon has written many training protocols and developed innovative training apparatuses. He is convinced that following protocols, collecting data, and educating trainers are all key to success. But even more important than these is removing traditional punishment training methods and replacing them with operant conditioning techniques. If you are interested in his seminars or workshops, please take a look at the website www.simon-prins.com.